Surviving Ireland

www.transworldireland.ie

www.transworldbooks.co.uk

Surviving Ireland

Colm Tobin

Illustrations by Ian Benjamin Kenny

TRANSWORLD IRELAND

TRANSWORLD IRELAND PUBLISHERS
28 Lower Leeson Street, Dublin 2, Ireland
www.transworldireland.ie

Transworld Ireland is part of the Penguin Random House group of companies
whose addresses can be found at global.penguinrandomhouse.com

First published in the UK and Ireland in 2015
by Transworld Ireland
an imprint of Transworld Publishers

A CIP catalogue record for this book
is available from the British Library.

ISBN 9781848272132

Typeset in 11½/15½pt Minion Pro by Falcon Oast Graphic Art Ltd.

Printed and bound in Great Britain by Clays Ltd, St Ives plc

Penguin Random House is committed to a sustainable
future for our business, our readers and our planet. This book
is made from Forest Stewardship Council® certified paper.

MIX
Paper from
responsible sources
FSC® C018179

1 3 5 7 9 10 8 6 4 2

Contents

Foreword

I t's exhausting. Being Irish. The weight of history. The self-doubt. The constant analysis. The wind.

You'd sometimes wonder why we are so hard on ourselves. Is it the post-colonial overhang following centuries of oppression at the hands of a litany of foreign invaders? Or could it be the collective guilt and deep shame we feel for having sent Westlife out into the wider world?

Perhaps we're just bored?

In Ireland, navel-gazing has become a national sport. If our current-affairs TV shows aren't repeatedly raking over scandals from the past, they are horrifying us with portents of the doom to come, stoking up fear about all the horrors and misfortunes that are surely only around the corner. In the run-up to 2016, we have been in danger of entering a whole new golden age of rabid self-reflection. We've already been inundated with an unprecedented array of debates on the nature of Irishness and on what it truly means to be Irish. We've already seen the unedifying scraps between historians, the ceremonial hijackings by political parties and those endless documentaries with tuba-heavy soundtracks featuring grey-haired men spouting misty-eyed horseshit, each of them visibly laden down by the overbearing weight of their own accumulated opinions.

This book is basically my attempt to get on the ladder before everyone else. Designed to act as a survival guide for anyone living in or visiting the country, over the course of these chapters I will attempt to unmask the real Ireland. What is the true essence of this mysterious mist-green land with its majestic, undulating landscape so battered by harsh winds and the angry seas that spit and fizz and churn? Is there anything to be said about this little island – with its jagged, teddy-bear outline, which lurks guiltily to the western edge of Europe as if it were illegally parked – that hasn't already been summed up neatly on TV adverts for rashers? And what of the creatures who live here? What can we say about the tribes that have formed and the lives that they lead? Can the Irish be defined as the slick, upwardly mobile, bright young things of Europe with the skinny jeans and the unnecessary spectacles? Or are they still the slack-jawed simpletons staring toothlessly out of John Hinde postcards, patting their donkeys and waiting patiently for death? Is it possible that there is a third, or even a fourth, category of Irish person? Also why, for instance, are we still known as 'the land of saints and scholars' when recent history would suggest we are primarily made up of below-average accountants and people who are handy with the greyhounds?

Irishness means more than merely holding a passport with a harp on it. It has an international resonance, enjoyed annually by millions the world over as they strap on fake red beards and parade themselves silly in novelty leprechaun hats before proudly raising a pint glass to our patron saint, ~~Arthur~~ Patrick. Some say you can hear Irishness in the lonesome lilt of the uilleann pipes. That you can smell it on the farts of a billion Guinness drinkers. Look hard enough and they say you can see it winking back at you from the oily thighs of Michael Flatley.

As you will find out, most of this is bollocks.

You see, Ireland is no longer just a physical place. Through emigration we have transcended space and time by spitting people out in all directions, over the course of many generations, particularly those too talented and troublesome to be left around the place. What can we say about the scattered millions of the diaspora? Are we happy to leave them to rot away in the bedsits of London or at the all-night beach orgies of Bondi? Or are we right to harness their global influence and their creative energy by bringing them back home and shaking them down for cash, like we did a few years back during The Gathering?

Over the following chapters I will attempt to answer at least some of these questions without getting too distracted by Facebook.

Surviving Ireland is designed as a handbook to modern Irish life and although primarily aimed at an Irish-born audience, I hope it will also be read and enjoyed by people the world over, including the following:

- Recently sworn-in Irish citizens
- Visiting tourists
- Richard and/or Judy
- Drunk people in airports buying it by mistake, thinking it's the latest novel from Colm Tóibín

I hope you enjoy it.

Colm Tobin

Chapter 1

Climate

In **Ireland,** no subject occupies our day-to-day conversation like the weather. It is a constant wellspring of drama. Nothing stays the same for long. Dramatic winds can pick up on the calmest of afternoons. Cold, rain-soaked mornings suddenly turn hot and humid. Scorching summer days can veer off and turn wet and nasty.

The truth is, in a country where the folk memory of civil war lingers in our subconscious, where the collective wounds from Saipan still lie open and exposed, it is vital to have something non-controversial to blather on about. The weather does exactly that job.

So, to prepare you for life in Ireland, let's look at some of the main categories of Irish weather, beginning with the most common of them all – the rain.

The Rain

If the rain in Spain falls mainly on the plain, then the rain in Ireland falls mainly on . . . well, the Irish.

Ireland is chiefly famous the world over for two things – being green and being wet. It's slightly unfair. The truth is, eastern counties only experience about 150 wet days per year. That's a lot of dry days in between. Admittedly, for some western areas this figure shoots up to 225 wet days. On rare sunny days in Castlebar, it is not uncommon to see pale and shocked locals staring skywards at the sun and applauding.

We all know that rain can be disastrous. It can soak into you and sit around on the skin, inviting in all sorts of plagues and illnesses. It can mockingly destroy the impromptu plans of barbecue organizers. It laughs in the face of race meetings, making the going 'soft-heavy in places'. Believe me, there's nothing worse than when the going is soft-heavy in places for a horse in a hurry.

We have numerous adjectives with which to describe it – lashing, pissing, bucketing . . . if the Inuits have fifty words for snow, the Irish have about a hundred variations of 'Bollocks, I'm after getting soaked'.

So, in order to keep you as safe and dry as possible, here's a small compendium of the various categories of rain to watch out for.

Irish people should have evolved some sort of umbrella arm by now.

Stage 1: 'Tis a Grand Soft Day, Thank God

Gorgeously atmospheric, soft day rain is best experienced around the mountainous, coastal fringes of the west of Ireland. A subtle cross between mist and drizzle, soft day rain is a mysterious and subtle form of precipitation. For the first ten minutes of contact, it appears benevolent and feels like it is having no great impact. You might even chance going out without a coat. It's refreshing, almost. Unfortunately, before you know it, you'll be wetter than a film with Hugh Grant in it.

We all know the soggy horror of being caught outside on a dank, miserable, wet, muggy, damp, slippery, moist, misty, soaking, drizzly, sloppy fucker of a day.

Wetness: Low at first, very high eventually

Stage 2: Spitting

Spitting rain is the small nagging child of precipitation. Although it won't wet you entirely, spitting rain has evolved cunning ways of getting at you – it tends to creep along the forehead and enter the eyeballs at odd angles. It splashes up from the ground and attacks the sock and ankle area with a great and unexpected tenacity. It can mysteriously appear on the underside of umbrellas even though the top is bone dry. It can be a complete nightmare for drivers trying to decide on an appropriate wiper setting. Note that it's pronounced 'shpitting'.

Wetness: Fair to middlin'

Stage 3: Regular Rain

Regular Irish rain is the most straightforward example of precipitation. It truly is the working class of the water cycle. Visible to the naked eye, honest in the manner in which it descends from the sky, unpretentious to a fault . . . regular rain is sound. Of course, like any rain, it can soak you to the skin if unprepared, but you were probably asking for it.

Wetness: Light if well prepared; severe if you act the spanner

Stage 4: Lashing

When it's lashing, it's no laughing matter. It doesn't just rain cats and dogs. Cows, zebras, stoats and sloths have often been observed. When it's lashing, you may stay indoors.

It's true that lashing rain can be a wonderful thing, e.g. when it's beating off the window and you're snuggled up by the stove with a book like you're in an ad for Dulux Weathershield. But not if you're outside. I've seen grown men sitting in the middle of the street, defeated by lashing rain; puddles forming around their shivering bodies, praying that someone might come along and shoot them in the face.

Wetness: Severe

Stage 5: Bucketing Down

Bucketing rain can elicit startled observations in open-plan offices. 'Jesus, it's fucking biblical!' You know it's serious when Irish people begin to openly express concern about rainfall. Going out in biblical rain is not advisable and can lead to unfortunate outcomes, e.g. death. However, one of the wonderful side effects of bucketing-down rain is a little-known phenomenon called rain euphoria. Rain euphoria occurs when you get so completely and utterly soaked that you begin to mysteriously enjoy the experience. People with rain euphoria can be seen skipping down streets, lepping into water fountains, swinging off lamp posts and ripping their clothes off, all the while laughing maniacally into the clouds.

Wetness: *So wet it's funny*

Stage 6: Limerick Rain

Very little is known by the wider population about Limerick rain but it is one of the meteorological wonders of the world. Sure, typhoons, hurricanes and tsunamis grab the headlines for their dramatic and destructive impact – huge physical events that rip through cities in front of your eyes. Limerick rain, by contrast, causes its destruction over a longer period and in a much more insidious, parasitic manner. In Limerick, they don't have dry spells, instead they say 'The rain is waiting'.

Limerick rain is unique in that, on average, it falls for up to 378 days per year. Not only that, but it can defy physics and pass through barriers. It's not uncommon, for example, to be lying in bed in Annacotty and the rain mysteriously begins cascading from the ceiling. In fact, Limerick is the only place in the world where it is known to rain regularly indoors. There is nothing unusual about a family gathered around the TV on a Saturday evening watching *The X Factor* under an umbrella.

It doesn't end there, however. Limerick rain has a horrifying, almost supernatural intelligence. It seeps through gable walls like the magician David Copperfield, creeps up into crevices, defying gravity and making a mockery of modern waterproofing technology. It laughs in the face of oilskins. When Limerick rain falls on your head, it doesn't stop at the skin. It slowly soaks into the brain, starting at the stem, seeping up through the cerebellum, spreading around both hemispheres, riddling the frontal lobe, where it sets about poisoning your very thoughts. It forms new neural networks that run like gutters in your thinking. You can see the effects of Limerick rain on the streets – people shouting 'Shitfuckbollocks!' for no apparent reason, old women trying to shift the statue of Paul O'Connell, crows flinging themselves into electricity pylons just to end the unrelenting wetness. Limerick rain destroys careers and breaks up marriages. It causes untold anguish before flowing out of the sockets of your eyes and the orifices of your ears, dragging with it any store of happiness you had built up in your childhood. In all honesty, Limerick rain is more like Ebola than a meteorological event.

But at least it's not as bad as sideways rain.

Wetness: Not measurable using current instrumentation

Stage 7: Sideways Rain

Sideways rain combines two of the worst things about living in Ireland. The wind and the rain. It is truly an elemental cluster-fuck. Sideways rain usually sweeps across your torso like a samurai sword, ripping into your guts and shearing the very skin from your cheeks. Sideways rain is almost impossible for a person to fend off. Although Limerick rain can invade your consciousness, you have some hope of escape (e.g. leaving Limerick). Sideways rain, on the other hand, attacks you in terrifying waves. If you are upended from the rear by sideways rain, it will wait for you to get to your feet before launching another full-frontal attack, knocking you on your arse again. If you attempt to get away, the wind and the rain will conspire to roll you around in mid-air, like a crocodile killing a pig. You really haven't a hope. The only appropriate response to sideways rain is to lie down and die, leaving all your worldly possessions to the rain.

Wetness: Catastrophic

Snowpocalypse

Ireland was covered in ice for centuries. The place was riddled with it. You could happily skate straight from Cork to Dublin in under a day. It got so cold in the midlands at this time they named a town Birr.

This glacial past forms an important part of the school curriculum. We all remember eskers, moraines, erratics, cirques, tarns and plucking from our geography classes. If all this wasn't enough, many Irish people spent much of the Celtic Tiger era skiing around the mountain ranges of Central Europe.

So you'd think we'd be fairly handy at dealing with the odd subzero foray on the old thermometer, right?

Wrong.

Sadly, Irish people deal with cold snaps with all the composure of a cat trying to escape from a bin liner.

It all begins in the way you'd expect. As the first few flakes fall, the country is overtaken with an understandably childlike excitement. Snotty-nosed youths leap out of windows, brandishing shovels, sleds and carrots. The sound of Aled Jones's 'Walking In The Air' echoes across the hilltops. Instagram servers go down as people gobble up bandwidth uploading photos of 'Snow on the road', 'Snow beside the road' and 'OMFG – there's snow on the bonnet of the car!!!'

The basic consensus is: holy living shit, it's not mild!

After the initial wave of euphoria, and because we are an enterprising people, we start to innovate ways to capitalize on the emerging chill. The first inevitably being – can we get off school/work?

It's sobering to remember that in Canada, houses become completely engulfed by snowfalls as temperatures plunge, in one record case down to –63 degrees Celsius. Canadian children will regularly travel alone through blizzards and have to fight bears to receive their education. In Ireland, when a light dusting of snow falls, we begin to issue nanny-state health-and-safety edicts to prevent kids leaving the house.

Inevitably, channelling the sombre tones of Winston Churchill circa The Blitz, the Minister for Snow will be wheeled out, usually on a brand-new set of winter tyres.

Minister for Snow: *All schools will be closed from tomorrow morning and probably for the rest of the week pending a review by myself, the rest of An Bord Sneachta and Evelyn Cusack.*

Media person: *Why?*

Minister for Snow: *In case an unfortunate accident occurs, like a rogue snowball bringing down a helicopter or a paedophile snowman entering a school.*

Media person: *And what are you proposing to do about the state of the roads?*

Minister for Snow: *The army will break up the roads with kango hammers and throw them in the sea. This should prevent skidding, sliding, slipping or any other lateral vehicular movement on the ice. Anyone caught skidding willy-nilly 'for fun' will be taken out and shot between the shoulder blades.*

Media person: *And what about the elderly?*

Minister for Snow: *The elderly and infirm will be set on fire to keep the rest of us warm.*

Media person: *But . . .*

Minister for Snow: *No further questions. Break a leg!*
(fires snowball)

The entire country, if you'll pardon the expression, has a bit of a meltdown.

It's not just the schools either. Everything stops. Bridges are left levitating as workers scarper off home. Heart transplants are abandoned mid-incision. Fourth-year A-student undergrads drop out of college and start voraciously injecting heroin.

It's less like a minor weather event and more like an end-of-days snowmageddon. Raw panic ensues. News camera crews inflict hernias on themselves as they rush to talk to children in that patronizing way that news camera crews talk to children. And there's one topic of discussion, the most pressing issue of the moment, which just won't go away . . .

Media person: *(panicked) Have we enough salt, Minister?*

Minister for Snow: *I am fully satisfied that we have enough salt going forward. We have fifteen warehouses full of salt left over since the bad winter of 2010.*

Media person: *(more panicked) But what if we run out?*

Minister for Snow: *Don't you worry your little head, there's a container ship en route from Mogadishu with enough salt to preserve the townspeople of Athlone for a generation. And they'll throw in some vinegar as well just for you! Hup!*

Media person: *(extremely panicked now, frothing) But what if the ship sinks? Won't we all just skid into each other and die? WILL ALL THE AUSTERITY HAVE BEEN FOR NOTHING?!!!*

Minister for Snow: *Now, get a hold of yourself! Don't forget, we have another warehouse full of Joe Jacob's iodine tablets. And the e-voting machines give out great heat. But these are worst-case scenarios. Let's not lose the run of ourselves here. (fires snowball)*

Inevitably, like all the modern-day media storms, the cold snap passes, some salt gets spread on the roads, a man falls on the ice and becomes an international Internet celebrity, the schools reopen and we all go back to complaining about the bland, never-ending mildness of it all.

Surviving a Heatwave

It takes light about eight minutes to reach us from the sun. These brave light rays plunge heroically through almost 150 million kilometres of empty space, bending around planets, bouncing off asteroids, narrowly avoiding comets before they eventually reach the atmosphere above Ireland, where they bounce off the clouds and back up into space.

However, on those rare occasions when the sun makes it through, everything changes on the ground. One warm summer's day can lift the mood of the nation, putting a spring in our steps, a glint in our eyes and an ice cream in our hands. Indeed there's probably no sight happier than a fat little farmer emerging from a petrol station with a 99. This, to me, is the first sign of summer.

But the Irish mindset is complex. Even after only a few hours of sunshine, we begin to catastrophize about how it might all go pear-shaped. We have flashbacks to November gales and January floods. The fear sets in. Some people even start willing it to pour down, nervously announcing, 'We could do with a drop of rain,' as if they suffer from some sort of meteorological Stockholm syndrome.

So, in order to survive and navigate any unexpected heatwaves in your area, here are a number of simple tactics you can employ.

Beach Etiquette

Arrive early to find a good spot. As we will learn later, Irish people have a weird relationship with land and property, so it's best to get on the ladder early. Fire your towel on the sand to mark your territory before preparing the scaffolding for your elaborate arrangement of windbreakers.

Run right into the water. It is the only way to enter the sea around Ireland. Few sights are more tragic than that of porcelain-white Paddies nervously dipping their toes in the freezing ocean before running back to the safety of land with that pained expression like they've been stabbed with a bayonet. This flirtation can go on and on for hours, like some extended Beckettian farce. Just do it already.

When returning from your dip it is important to remember to almost walk into the faces of every sunbather lying in your path. They will appreciate the cooling effect of second-hand seawater falling into their eyes.

Always shake the sand out of your towel upwind of the nearest sunbather. People love nothing more than a mouthful of sand recently removed from the insides of your thighs.

What to Wear

Irish women generally have the summer fashion thing down. There will be enough summer dresses to populate a Bruce Springsteen song and it'll all be exceptionally tasteful. But Irish men are different. Sunshine seems to make us think we've been granted a 'licence to be wacky'. Most think it's appropriate to swan around like a cross between John Candy and Patrick Star from *SpongeBob SquarePants*, a hideous cocktail of Bermuda shorts and bad sandals. You'd be forgiven for thinking there'd been a fire at the circus.

Maybe tone it down a bit there lads.

Managing Expectations

Irish people can become disoriented in the early days of summer. There are so many false dawns and broken promises and, let's face it, we've all been hurt in the past.

A brave and bold move to wear shorts to the office can suddenly look very foolish. The sight of a rain-soaked Irish person in shorts sloshing around town can highlight man's folly more poignantly than any image of the sunken *Titanic*. So hedge your bets. Pack sunglasses, wellingtons, sun cream, umbrella, shorts and skis (more on this in Chapter 2). Even if, in your head, you are cartwheeling through St Stephen's Green with an almond Magnum in your gob, there's always a danger that the next minute you'll be cowering in a duffel coat in some rainy back alley faster than you can say *Angela's Ashes*.

Where to Go

Apart from the beach, there are a number of other options on a sunny day. One of the most popular is drinking outdoors, whether in a sun-filled beer garden or, say, the cricket lawns of the Pav at Trinity College. Be very careful, however. Many make their move too early in the day. An innocent 'Sure, we'll have one or two' at lunchtime can turn nasty by early evening. By then, you can see revellers sprawled across parks, like pigs full of cider, slowly cooking in their own juices. Pace yourselves.

Sunscreen

As you well know, it's vital to protect yourself against those UV rays. The wide range of sunscreen of varying factors should work for most people. Remember to protect the top of the nose.

The Seven Stages of the Irish Heatwave

The farmer's tan is one thing, but you don't want to end up walking around the place like Alex Ferguson twinned with Rudolph.

The truth is, most poor Irish souls just haven't been designed for any sort of exposure to the sun. Thanks to many millennia of hiding in holes from the British, our skin has not evolved to deal well with intense UV exposure. I once knew an Offaly man so fair-skinned he had to trowel on sun cream until he began to resemble one of those Pompeii body casts. During barbecues, we would have to carry him outdoors like a statue, lean him against the corner of a shed and feed him chopped-up burger meat with a plastic spoon.

For others, more conscious of their appearance, a spray-on tan usually works best. These vary from the subtle to the nuclear orange. The more extreme shades are the reason Dublin city centre looks like an Oompa Loompa colony late on a Saturday night. So don't overdo it.

The Wind

If Bob Dylan was right and the answer is blowing in the wind, you'd think someone in Ireland would have heard it by now.

It's fair to say that the winds of Ireland have made their mark on the land and on the people. You can see them whipping across the surface of the North Atlantic, churning up waves and flinging hapless surfers into the watery depths of Sligo Bay. You can even see their signature edged into the worn and beaten foreheads of auld fellas at race meetings, with their perpendicular hair, like they're playing opposite Celine Dion in a music video.

In order to keep you fully alert to these squally and

potentially dangerous conditions, I've prepared this handy chart, with a little help from Mr Beaufort.

The Winds of Ireland

Force 1 Calm — Not a puff

Force 2 Light air — Smoke goes a bit bendy

Force 3 Light breeze — Wind felt on face

Force 4 Moderate breeze — Wind scatters sensitive files and brown envelopes

Force 5 Fresh breeze — Trees sway, cheeks redden, there's great drying out

Force 6 Strong breeze — Whistling heard in telephone lines, eyebrows start to go stupid

Force 7 Near gale — Elderly men at GAA matches struggle to read programmes, flags on poles go bananas

Force 8 Gale — Lads, we're not in Kansas any more

Force 9 Strong gale — Atheists start praying, slight structural damage to buildings/your face

Force 10 Storm — Farmyard animals/old ladies/farmyards seen flying past windows

Force 11 Violent storm — Aaaaaaaaaaaaaaaagh!

Force 12 Hurricane — Clocks stop working, entire life flashes before your eyes

Chapter 2

Essential Equipment

To have any hope of surviving modern Ireland, with its myriad dangers, pitfalls and trapdoors, not to mention sporadic outbreaks of the winter vomiting bug, it'll help to equip yourself with a very basic toolkit. These are the must-have items – you simply must not leave home without them.

WARNING: Failure to follow this advice could lead to any or all of the following within minutes:

- Foot-and-mouth disease
- Negative equity
- Death
- Being asked by a garda to 'Please, step outside the veh-hickle'

Wellies

Previously the preserve of tillage farmers and eccentric poets from Monaghan, wellies are now bang on trend for the entire population and can be enjoyed by young hipsters and old farmers alike. Indeed, a whole new generation of 'farmsters' has emerged in recent years.

This welly resurgence is due in large part to neopagan events like the Electric Picnic and because wankers in jeeps with keys attached to their belts kept building houses on flood plains during the Celtic Tiger. Thankfully, no multicoloured, polka-dot welly is too silly, no ironic, stencilled pattern is too naff and no price tag is too extortionate.

Tip: Make a bold statement by swaggering into a Sunday Mass service in dirty wellingtons. Nothing says 'pillar of the community' more confidently than someone casually dragging cow shit in around the altar.

Update: The Apple iWelly will come in three tones – green, orange and off-white – will function as a GPS-enabled fitness tracker running OS X 13.8 Himalayan Mountain Goat and you will even be able to use it to find your tent at festivals.

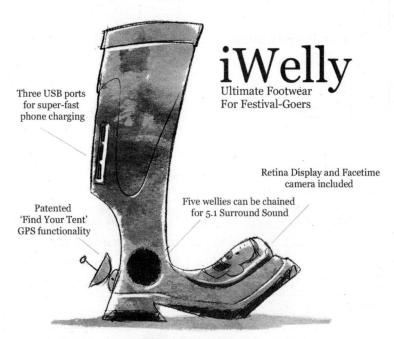

Three USB ports
for super-fast
phone charging

iWelly
Ultimate Footwear
For Festival-Goers

Retina Display and Facetime
camera included

Patented
'Find Your Tent'
GPS functionality

Five wellies can be chained
for 5.1 Surround Sound

Graphene sheen only two atoms thick (human faeces-resistant)

A Coat

As we have already learnt, Irish weather can vary from the mildly wet to the extremely wet and there are also sudden episodes of apocalyptic wetness, which are almost impossible to predict.

Do not be downhearted.

A wide range of outerwear exists to suit a variety of personalities: Penneys coats, duffel coats, overcoats, undercoats, ironic tweed West Brit landlord coats, coats with their own immersions, Údarás na Gaeltachta-subsidized Connemara coats with matching beards, Lycra coats for middle-aged fad joggers (with supporting beer-belly scaffolds) and vinyl hipster smoking jackets that play a wide back catalogue of rare Northern Soul on contact with a record needle.

Mobile Phone and Wallet

A vital part of modern Irish life, mobile phones are useful whether you are navigating around Sheep's Head using GPS, ordering rare pet spiders on the Internet or just passive-aggressively ignoring family members during Sunday dinner. Indeed, a recent survey on mobile-phone usage in Ireland found that 67 per cent of Irish people taking the survey weren't in fact paying any attention to the survey at all because they were apathetically scrolling through Facebook at the time, endlessly clicking and liking and throwing sheep, but all the while dreaming, deep, deep down in the depths of their souls, dreaming that maybe this dystopian horror might one day end, so that they could return to the fields once again and play in the sunshine.*

* May be a subjective interpretation of the survey.

Another thing, bring a wallet. Seriously. Ireland is expensive. We owe over five hundred thousand million trillion euros to a bunch of glorified Bond villains called the Troika. Hence, buying a pint in some parts of Temple Bar can cost more than an average black-market kidney. There is also the constant neediness of the government, relentlessly pulling at your arm like a five-year-old child looking for sweets – taxing fuel, tolling the roads, charging for water that falls out of the sky for free anyway, putting surcharges on this, excise on that, government duty on the other, secretly pulling your teeth out at night while you sleep ... So if you don't have a nice fat wallet, and it gives me no pleasure to say this, you'll be about as useful here as Ronan Keating at an opera festival.

Selfie Stick

It is vital nowadays to photographically catalogue every single moment of your life, from the beginning to the end, either for storage or instant publication on social media. In fact, it is easy to end up feeling a bit like a Japanese tourist documenting for posterity some endlessly unfolding holiday.

The filtered Instagramming of everything – from the food we consume to the children we produce to the wakes we gate-crash – is simply a part of the modern life experience. Every milestone on the journey needs to be published as a sort of mini-press release to friends and strangers alike, carefully hinting why you are in fact that little bit better and more successful than them.

Neatly, a selfie stick also doubles as a walking stick on mountainous terrain and can even be employed to hunt loose cattle on your path while shouting 'Sook sook sook sook sook sook', which is apparently how you must speak to cattle.

The Constitution

No, I'm not talking about carrying around a copy of the actual Constitution. Nobody does that, apart from Michael D. Higgins and the odd Supreme Court judge. The rest of us really only need to know 'the spirit' of the Irish constitution – which is '*Omne bonum*' or 'It'll be grand'.

What I mean is that there's no point living in Ireland if you don't have the constitution for it. You see, the Irish constitution is a medical anomaly. Physicians talk a lot about the 'French paradox', the observation of low coronary heart disease death rates despite high intake of dietary cholesterol and saturated fat among French people, however, this pales in comparison to the 'Irish question', which basically states 'How on earth are you actually still alive?'

So, ask yourself this: could you handle a four-course meal involving mostly carbohydrates, thirty-five varieties of potato, a fatty cut of sumptuous mountain lamb the size of a small tractor followed by jelly and ice cream and a large cappuccino smothered in chocolate? Could you then follow this by 'a feed of pints', a small plate of hang sangwiches and a packet of Bacon Fries? If not, I would honestly consider Japan.

A Working Liver

As well as a hardy constitution, a hard-working liver is absolutely essential. Binge drinking, as we will find out later, is a national sport and our collective relationship with alcohol is about as healthy as Gollum's relationship with rings. So, make sure to have your body primed for an assault on every single orifice. Start by slowly introducing alcohol into your daily diet – a nip of whiskey here, a flagon of cider there – and, before you know it, you'll be problem-drinking to beat the band! Be sure to build this up slowly over a couple of months though. Would you run a marathon without training?

No, you would not.

A Strong Neck

In Ireland, it helps to have 'neck for rope'. This means having a, on the face of it, cheeky disposition and penchant for cutting corners/flouting the rules, but what in reality amounts to a Machiavellian ability to get ahead and sure, fuck the consequences. If you don't believe me google 'Mahon Tribunal'.

Not everyone is born with a strong neck, but absolutely anyone can develop one. Start by engaging in small-scale activities like sticking chewing gum to the underside of tables or tailgating fellow citizens to avoid paying motorway tolls. Before you know it you'll be living the dream as a successful rogue solicitor selling dubious Bulgarian property off plans to gullible relatives. Or even making a name for yourself in local politics.

The English Language

Irish is the official language of Ireland but, in practice, it is about as widely used these days as asbestos. Instead, English is more widely spoken, although there are certain parts of Georgian Dublin where Latin still holds sway. The English used in the rest of Ireland is a version that do be called Hiberno-English. People that do try to explain Hiberno-English in books like this often make a pure hames of it and I have an awful shtrain on me, trying to think of ways to do it. You'd be driven out of your mind from it. Anyway, I'm half banjaxed after writing the rest of the chapter so we'll move away on.

Chapter 3

The Plain People of Ireland

M ost Irish people are weary yet forgiving when it comes to our wanton stereotyping around the globe. This imagery pops up every now and again and it is at best lazy and at worst catastrophically offensive. Children on the backs of piebald ponies dashing through ghost estates, homeless finance ministers begging for cash in the streets, leprechauns getting in over their heads in Middle Eastern property consortiums . . . You'd have to bite your tongue at times.

But we've all got blood on our hands. The stereotypes within the island of Ireland are just as lazy: the racist Dublin taxi driver, the mean Cavan bastard, the cute Cork hoor, the eccentric District Court judge, the heavy metal-loving Offaly lorry driver . . .

The truth of contemporary Ireland is very different. We are a diverse, creative and modern people, comfortable in a globalized, technological world and eager to engage with the other occupants of planet earth, often by hustling drunk Americans in online chess late at night.

One of the best places to see the whole breadth of Irish life is in that great contemporary church, the motorway services area. Here you will see them in all their glory, like wildlife parading the African savannah: school tours and bickering families, travelling salesmen and vans full of criminals in transit, all stuffing their faces with hash browns, poring over tabloids and often dashing towards the jacks with a worried wincing.

Who are these people?

Pat, 56, Pig Farmer, Monaghan

Like many Irish farmers, Pat has had to diversify his income streams over recent years and he has really embraced tech-nology in order to do this. Although his first love is still the farm (he even names his cows and cried for ten minutes last week after sending Scarlett Johansson to the slaughter-house), Pat has also launched a number of quirky, innovative sideline projects. These include IrishAir.org, where he sells bottles of fresh, recently captured pig-farm air on the Internet, mostly to foreigners and culchies exiled in Dublin. Frustrated by the slow roll-out of rural broadband, Pat went ahead and bought his own bandwidth on the Astra satellite last October, becoming a significant player in the Russian telecoms market by mistake.

Pat is in services today buying a *Farmer's Journal* and a party bag of Skittles.

Móna, 37, Teacher, Dublin

Móna is originally from Termonfeckin but left in the early nineties because, well, because Termonfeckin. Móna is, on the face of it, just another friendly presence in the staffroom, but in truth she is hiding a secret from her colleagues, namely that she has been happily living with her partner Laura for over a decade now.

Móna is in services today having a poo.

Assumpta, 13, Computer Programmer, Tubbercurry

Assumpta taught herself to code online during the bad winter of 2010 when she was eight. She has since launched thirty-two apps across iPhone and Android devices and is thought to have a net worth of over three billion dollars. Assumpta also enjoys swimming and camogie.

Assumpta is in services today on a school trip to Dublin. She just picked up a Walnut Whip and a copy of the *Financial Times*.

Oisín, 28, Student, Wicklow

Oisín is a postgraduate student in Trinity College Dublin. He is currently working on his master's thesis 'Deconstructing tetra-sexual linguistics: vampire theory and masturbation in post-feminist Japanese anime'. Oisín is a member of the Socialist Workers Party on campus and spends much of his free time leafleting and raising awareness for what he sees as the slow erosion of the welfare state by the international neoliberal elite. This is particularly relevant to his life given that he's been illegally on the scratch while studying for well over five years now. Oisín will be the first to admit that he hasn't got it all figured out yet, but like many other dangerous sociopaths, he is likely to do very well in academia.

Oisín is in services today with his daddy, who just gave him four hundred euros towards rent and is driving him back to Dublin, where he will go on a water protest.

Modhidharma, 57, Reiki Healer, Allihies, West Cork

Modhidharma (Buddhist name meaning all-pervading peace mother; real name Pauline) was originally from Devon in the UK and ran a successful mortgage brokerage in London during Thatcher's reign in the eighties, when she simply went by her birth name, Pauline Chiles. After her second divorce, Modhidharma finally escaped the rat race in 1988, moving to rural West Cork in order to find herself/stop taking so much cocaine. Modhidharma now juggles a career in massage therapy and reiki healing and like many English people living in West Cork, she has had some minor success as a video artist. Modhidharma has an exclusively sexual relationship with a 22-year-old local fisherman called Fachtna, who has massive hands.

Modhidharma is in services for the first time ever today, returning from a weekend-long transcendental meditation retreat at a Buddhist centre in Nobber. Despite three days filled with deep calm and mindfulness, the only thing Modhidharma can think about is burning this terrible shithole to the ground with everyone in it.

Mikey, 2, Boy Racer, Letterkenny

Like many two-year-olds and, indeed, Donegal people, Mikey spends much of his time mumbling away in a dialect known only to himself while other people look on cooing and smiling. Mikey is notable in that he is a seasoned boy racer, having crashed his first car aged eight and a half months.

Mikey is in services today on the way to Mondello Park with his brother 'Cheetah' Andy. They just stocked up on Red Bull.

Jonathan, 43, Taxi Driver, Rush

Jonathan is originally from Nigeria and became an Irish citizen in 2012, not because of any particularly deep love for Ireland, but because of a deep fear of going back to Nigeria. Jonathan is a taxi driver in Dublin, having spent two years previously working for tips in the downstairs toilet of a hip Dublin late bar. Here he mostly dealt with drunken Celtic Tiger monsters repeatedly asking 'Where are you from in Africa?' before saying something complimentary about the intelligent play of Didier Drogba. He eventually saved up enough money to go into business ferrying the same vomiting idiots around the city every weekend. Pretty miraculously, after all that, Jonathan still quite likes Irish people.

He is in services today buying diesel and picked up some trucker's socks even though he didn't particularly need them.

Ned, 63, Professional Aul' Lad, Bandon

Ned is scientifically notable as one of the most bored people on the planet. A recent study by sociologists in University College Cork found Ned's heart rate to be almost imperceptible – he is clinically just above comatose – yet he still manages to perform his day-to-day activities, namely walking the short distance down from his house to the local bridge where he will sit for hours and hours staring at passing traffic. Sometimes he is joined by his old schoolmate Tim, who will sit and stare at the cars with him, their heads turning in deep, unspoken synchronicity, like dolphins on display at SeaWorld. Ned and Tim haven't exchanged a raw syllable since 1972.

Ned is in services today on his way to a greyhound meeting in Portlaoise, the first time he has left Bandon in over a decade. He just bought himself a box of spicy wedges.

Wallace, 38, Zeitgeist Manipulator, Camden Street, Dublin

Wallace is a successful copywriter and brand manager with a digital sales optimization agency called Bluffr. He lives alone in a converted mews property in Dublin's south inner city, which sports a minimalist interior design inspired by Japanese electronica and has the hexadecimal colour #CCFFFF as a central unifying theme. Wallace's wood-burning stove takes pride of place at the centre of the high-ceilinged central space, efficiently radiating heat, which rises high up into the rafters (mingling as it does with Wallace's own quiet sense of self-satisfaction, which itself pervades the property like some preening invisible cat). Little does he know it, but in recent months two of Wallace's friends have genuinely fantasized about murdering him at different dinner parties he's hosted in his well-appointed gaff (BER rating A2). His PA Monica playfully thought about chopping him up with a meat cleaver and disposing of his remains in a remote wasteland on 18 September during a particularly one-sided conversation they were having about avant-jazz. Only this July, his 'best friend' Andy methodically planned through all the logistical details of disembowelling Wallace using the ancient Inuit hunting tool that dangles in his well-lit staircase (capturing as it does the evening sun, before flinging it in shards across the kitsch veneer-panelling of his airy landing). Andy pictured himself finishing off the job by stuffing Wallace's limp corpse into the same wood-burning stove before setting it alight, in some sort of primitive, ironic sacrifice. It goes without saying that neither Monica nor Andy are bad people and neither would ever follow through on these fantasies, but the thoughts themselves go in some way to illustrate the sort of Serie A-level arsehole we are dealing with here.

Wallace is in services today on his way to spend a night alone in an Airbnb cottage in Connemara, where he will scroll through Instagram for hours and drink two bottles of wine. He was miffed and irritated when he learnt they didn't stock the *Observer*.

Esther, 31, Musician, Galway

Struggling singer-songwriter Esther has been living in Galway ever since dropping out of an arts degree in UCG during the mid-noughties. Esther has been going steady with Dave, a barman, for well over a decade and they share an apartment overlooking a large building that overlooks a hotel that overlooks the harbour. Esther is prone to flights of fantasy, great bouts of emoting and moments of inspired passion, all of which pop up in the lyrics of her three self-released acoustic albums, the latest of which, *A Kind Of Sadness*, received a three-star review in *Hot Press*. Esther loves woolly hats and tea, warm fires and cute dogs, and sometimes she cries to herself when she thinks of the early death of Nick Drake. When Esther looks into Dave's eyes she imagines torrents of passion rising and falling like great waves; she can envisage whole universes beginning and ending, days rising and nights falling. When Dave looks into Esther's eyes he wishes he could see someone who contributed anything at all towards the electricity bill.

Esther is in services today to buy an absolute fuckload of chocolate.

Colm, 21, Comedy Writer, The Internet

Colm has been sitting in the café section of services now for over four hours, observing the passing customers for a section in a new humour book he is writing about contemporary Ireland, based on a Twitter persona he developed by accident, and which will be predominantly read by people sitting on toilets. Although he's enjoying the process of writing, because, let's be honest, it's about time he did something with his life, Colm wonders, deep down, if the fact that he's getting paid to sit here today making sarcastic observations about regular people, people he can truly know nothing about, and who are just going about their daily lives in as honourable a way as they can, could in some way represent the very death of culture.

Colm has bought and consumed six cups of coffee in services today and his eyeballs look like they might try to escape his skull at any moment.

Veronica, 23, Future Taoiseach, Meath

Veronica is a member of Young Fine Gael, one of the few organizations in the world whose name survives despite being a fully functioning oxymoron. The truth is, although there are, technically, young people in Fine Gael, none of them are young in the way you and I understand the word. You see, Veronica, even though she's aged twenty-three, has a spiritual age of around seventy-six.

Veronica will regularly walk around the campus of Belfield (where she is doing a degree in agricultural science) with the theme from *The West Wing* going round in her head. Often, on her way to meetings of the Young Fine Gael branch in the arts block, she'll pretend to be doing a security detail on the building, her hand to her pretend earpiece, dutifully overseeing security checks on all the entrances with her crack team of imaginary African-American special agents. At lunch she will often perform 'walk and talks', playing the roles of both POTUS *and* Secretary of State, and will often centre these conversations around international crises involving the Chinese or what she might need to pick up in Spar for dinner. Although Veronica seems relatively harmless, and a little bit of a joke to her fellow ag-science students, they should pay heed, as she will almost certainly be running the country within a decade.

Veronica is in services today to pick up a copy of *The Phoenix* magazine, which she finds pure gas altogether.

Jimmy, 71, Retired Teacher, Wexford

Jimmy is mad as hell and he's not going to take it any more. A retired geography teacher, Jimmy spent much of his youth with a vaguely leftist outlook on the world, mostly inspired by the folk music of Pete Seeger and Woody Guthrie. As he entered his thirties and settled down, Jimmy's politics shifted to a more pragmatic right-of-centre position, advocating free-market capitalism as the best of a bad lot and, like most Irish teachers of his generation, was a paper millionaire by the year of his retirement. In 2009, Jimmy lost much of his savings on

47

supposedly blue-chip AIB bank shares and a Bulgarian apartment that he bought off-plan and never got built. A month later he grew his hair long for the first time in over three decades and bought a Harley-Davidson with what little money he had left in his savings. Like many people his age, Jimmy now doesn't give a flying fuck, so much so that he would now consider himself a full-blown anarchist.

Jimmy is making a pit stop at services to smoke a roll-up with all the youthful ferocity of James Dean. Later, Jimmy will storm the AGM of a supposed pillar bank where he will pelt the suited fuckers with those rotten eggs he's been keeping in his shed since Christmas.

Chapter 4

History

The history of Ireland is long and fraught and filled with many shades of pain, from deep tragedy and outright horror, right down to smaller niggles like sprained ankles that are usually easy enough to run off. What could go wrong often did go wrong, but then it got worse and just as things were about to pick up . . . someone fell off a cliff. The list of our accumulated disasters and misfortune includes famine, invasions, mass emigration, economic stagnation, gombeen politics, rampant institutional abuse and numerous failed insurrections, not to mention Tom Cruise's accent in *Far and Away*.

So why rake over all that? says you. Life is short and there are many other things you could be doing instead of dolefully mulling over the past. For example, you could be:

- Enjoying a relaxing bath
- Watching cat videos on the Internet
- Rotating in a swivel chair really fast
- Making up to $1000 a week working from home

But, as the old saying goes, those who fail to learn from Leaving Cert history are often condemned to repeat it. So, if you are to hold any chance of surviving this wonderful yet complex island, it is right and proper to at least attempt to become properly informed about its past.

With that in mind, and to save you all the bother of going to the library, or indeed looking anything up on Wikipedia, I've gathered together the most important and instructive moments here, a series of events that may help explain why the country is as we know it today – quite honestly, a little bit batshit.

The Break with Britain

The first major milestone in Irish history occurred when Europe was almost entirely covered in ice. No amount of Aran sweaters, Ovaltine or dry-wall insulation could have kept out the infernal cold. It was absolutely, although not literally, Baltic.

Luckily, as far as we know, it was also devoid of any people. All in all, apart from a few feisty bears, migrating birds and the odd abandoned Esso station, the whole country was one barren, windswept, desolate wasteland – not unlike the moon or modern-day Longford.

At this time, Ireland was physically part of continental Europe but by 12000 BC, the chunk of land now known as Ireland had separated itself entirely from Great Britain. So even though no human being was living there yet, the very rocks themselves couldn't bear the idea of being under the thumb of imperial oppression for one day longer. According to geological texts commissioned by Éamon de Valera after independence, the land of Ireland 'pulled back its glacial sheets in an historic moment of noble revolution, and, as if stirring the very underlying system of plate tectonics that was her God-given birthright, did she so boldly strike for her freedom'.

So begins the story of Britain and Ireland sitting side by

side, together and alone, like a glum bride and groom at some ill-advised arranged marriage.

It was never going to end well.

The Dawn of the Irish

Once created, Ireland became the subject of a slew of invasions. The first actual people to arrive in Ireland hit land around 8000 BC. Typically, these Mesolithic invaders came from Britain (sure where else?!). Landing into the area that is now Temple Bar, these British scumbags (or Irish people as we know them today) came over here and took all our land. They razed whole areas to the ground, uprooting native Irish vegetation that had been peacefully photosynthesizing for centuries. They felled trees and polluted marshes, basically laying waste to a whole swathe of pure Gaelic fauna.

Like most Irish (or British) people who go somewhere in a large group to enjoy the craic, they decided they might stay on for a while longer. So they did, for about ten and a half thousand years (and counting).

Migrants also arrived along the coast from North Africa and the Mediterranean, bringing with them the building blocks of sean-nós music, a strong seafaring culture and, most importantly, figs, which they mysteriously knew how to roll into tasty biscuits. Although relatively unsophisticated, these people also brought a modicum of culture and progress to proceedings. They were expert cereal farmers, utilizing a range of crops imported from the Iberian peninsula. These included common staples like wheat and barley as well as more exotic cereals, like the notoriously unreliable Coco Pop, which was famous for 'turning the land chocolatey'.

It is worth noting that the early Irish were very environmentally conscious. It is believed they created the Newgrange monument as a means of capturing light in order to store it underground for the winter. Unfortunately for them, they never invented the technology to free this light, which is why the caves and passages underneath Ireland, to this very day, are believed to be brighter than a Super Bowl half-time show.

Once the Irish were settled, they quickly established the country as a centre of excellence for not being English. To this end, they created their own unique Gaelic language and indigenous customs, including sports like hurling, traditional arts like fiddling and a unique form of cheeky fun often referred to as scutting or divilment. Scutting or divilment involves generally roguish behaviour, e.g. cattle tipping, putting lipstick on a pig or guaranteeing the debts of failed banking institutions with public money.

These early Irish were in essence New Age hippies – most of them came from Britain, they wore dreadlocks, adored magic mushrooms and put their trust in a lot of scientifically implausible bunkum we'd hardly fall for now, like sun worship and homeopathy. But don't be deceived; they were also highly innovative. Such was their passion for play and gambling, it is believed they were the first race to invent the wheel, which they created specifically to play a rudimentary form of *Winning Streak*.

They even had their own legal system, called Brehon law. This was ahead of its time in many respects – it treated women with a certain degree of fairness and even allowed divorce on certain grounds, e.g. if your husband turned out to be a bollocks. There are people today – most of whom live in Ranelagh and enjoy traditional music – who believe that Brehon law was wildly liberal, coming from some store of right-on Celtic wisdom that has subsequently been ripped apart by a repressive Roman Church. Given that Brehon law allowed men to hit their wives and treated harpists as nobles, it is unlikely that it was, in truth, all that liberal. Anybody who's spent an extended period alone with a harpist knows this only too well.

All in all though, this was a great time to be alive in Ireland – we lived on our own island, on our own terms, with our own unique laws, free from any foreign interference.

But then God arrived.

Christianity

Before Christianity, Irish people were total pagans – they never went to Mass, were known to move in with each other before getting married and if all that wasn't heathen enough, they worshipped a range of dodgy gods including Enya, the ancient goddess of multitracking, and Fergal, king of sheds.

But then, all of a sudden, a little Welsh dude called Saint Patrick arrived, staff in hand, 'Hate/Snakes' tattooed on his arse, and he set about spreading the message of 'One True God' through the country like it was chlamydia.

It was going to be a challenge, establishing a monotheistic church in a land where people were used to rutting around in the mud and picking insects off one another, both of which are far more fun than squeezing yourself into a narrow wooden pew every week for hours of solemn apologizing. But somehow, St Patty, as he was known to absolutely nobody, managed to pull it off. He began by getting rid of all the snakes, a shamelessly populist move that lasted all the way up to the Celtic Tiger. But Patrick also made a fortuitous discovery; all Irish men have a deep-seated, natural inclination towards the monastic life. Let me explain.

Give any contemporary Irish man the option of living in silence at the top of a stone tower, drinking Buckfast all day while filling in colouring books, what do you think the response would be? We'd all be clambering up the side of Skellig Michael, PlayStation 3s and home-brewing kits tucked under our arms, looking forward to a life of quiet and deep reflection/living in our own filth. All of this interspersed, of course, by occasional visits to the fridge in a dressing gown like Tony Soprano.

So, St Patrick simply had to open the doors of the monasteries and watch them fill up with eager recruits. We were a monastic

FC Barcelona, producing some of the very best in Europe: Saint Colmcille, who founded the Iona Institute on a small area of moral high ground near Merrion Square; Saint Angus, who went on to become the patron saint of steak butties; and Saint Brendan the Navigator, the first monk to break America.

Viking Ireland

The Vikings arrived in Christian Ireland with all the subtlety of Ziggy Stardust walking into Mass. They came on their flatpack longships with the big Viggo Mortensen heads on them. They ravaged, raped, plundered and burned stuff and then they plundered a bit more, just for shits and giggles.

According to historical data unearthed in Dublin's Wood Quay, the Vikings were all complete and utter rides, every last one of them. But they were also crafty devils and they showed this by mostly attacking at night when the Irish were off their faces on Buckfast. These midnight raids weren't like a match at Thomond Park, where you stand up and fight fair against your enemy. They were more like when you bend down at school to pick up a biro and somebody slices your arse with a ruler. Shneaky.

Eventually, many Irish kings, like Cerball mac Dúnlainge (who, incidentally, established King crisps and went on to wage a thirty-year war with Mr Tayto), got sick of having their sleep constantly interrupted and entered into alliances with these Vikings, making peace by bartering valuable items like gold brooches, leather belts and box sets of *The Killing*. Inevitably, despite their general Norse aggression and promises of Scandinavian-style universal healthcare, we assimilated the Vikings, in much the same way as we would later assimilate Jack Charlton.

In all fairness, it wasn't all take take take. They left us a small town called Dublin, as well as a more surprising by-product – Iceland (which looks the same as 'Ireland', apart from one letter). The truth is, many Vikings simply stopped off to steal Irish women and moved on to Iceland to settle down, because it had a better music scene. Thus began a genetic trail combining the windswept, heavily cheek-boned facial structure of hairy Vikings with the untamed buck-wild taspy of tempestuous Irish women. Which would also neatly explain Björk.

The Normans

According to historical sources, the twelfth century was all a bit *Game of Thrones* in Ireland. There were over-kingdoms and lesser kingdoms and under-kingdoms, there was lots of unnecessary nakedness and many people spoke in that weird Aidan Gillen accent that nobody can quite place. It was around this time too that all the trouble with the neighbours started.

Dermot MacMurrough, in a fairly typically 'Leinster' move, invited in Strongbow and his Norman forces to annoy the other kings and these forces basically rampaged through the entire country. They picked on horses, they cut out the tongues of Irish speakers and they left lots of bitchy little notes in B&B guestbooks like 'The fry was a little tepid!!!' and 'No fresh lilies in the bedroom?' It was the starting point for over eight hundred horrendous years of British occupation.

Occupation and Moral Victory

The Irish didn't just sit back and take it, however. We dug our heels in and resisted the forces of the Crown – secretly practising our religion at Mass rocks, defiantly speaking our native tongue at Irish college (where you could also practise using your tongue on the opposite sex) and heroically supporting Celtic instead of Rangers.

But we also rebelled, often with brute violence, and I will now detail some of the greatest of our many accumulated moral victories (but using the present tense, because that is how historians do it on the telly).

1641: The upper-class Catholic gentry take control of Ireland for a decade before eventually being defeated by notorious bellend Oliver Cromwell.

1798: This glorious failed rebellion is led by Theobald Wolfe Tone, founder of the United Irishmen and also the man behind the album *Sixty Thousand Irish Drinking Songs To Punch Your Brother's Face To.* The rebellion founders, however, when fourteen thousand French soldiers supplying weapons refuse to enter Bantry Bay because they claim the coffee there isn't up to scratch.

1831: West Clare man Podge McCarthy gets drunk on poitín and starts a rebellion on his own. It is quashed after six minutes, however, when he stumbles trying to mount a horse and falls head first into a heap of manure. He dies three days later from a broken heart/dysentery.

1845: One million Irish people die between 1845 and 1852 due to an unconventional collective effort to leave the British Empire by starving themselves. This is substantially worse than previous famines – the Garlic Cheese and Chips Famine of 1812, which only kills one man called Ronan; and the Dublin Bay Prawn Famine of 1824, which more or less wipes out the entire townsfolk of Sutton. During the Great Famine (which wasn't great, incidentally; in fact, if anything, it was a bit shit), Irish people die in huge numbers – in poorhouses and hovels and on the side of the road. Some eat rodents to stay alive, some eat each other and, tragically, at least one man eats himself by mistake. Those that do survive are forced to emigrate to America, often on notorious 'coffin ships', which operate under horrific conditions similar to many of today's budget airlines.

1916: The 1916 Rising fails after the parties involved cannot agree on an appropriate manner to mark the centenary of the event, should they win independence. Subsequently, the Brits make the rather poor decision to execute the leaders, leading Michael Collins to famously declare 'Don't make me angry, you wouldn't like me when I'm angry' or something to that effect. (Sorry, I couldn't find the film online.)

Independence and Civil War

After the Rising, the British were getting sick of dealing with the troublesome Irish. It was coming to that stage where the parents are called in and everyone mutually agrees it is probably best if the child finds another school. Independence was finally granted on 6 December 1921, when Lloyd George and Michael Collins were co-signatories to a treaty titled 'Michael Collins's Death Warrant', which had been suspiciously faxed through by Éamon de Valera the previous evening. Sadly, de Valera couldn't be there to sign it himself due to Christmas shopping commitments on 8 December.

What followed was a most brutal civil war. A conflict that ripped through the very fabric of society – brother fought against brother, sister fought against sister, aunties randomly headbutted uncles over breakfast, sons-in-law delivered uppercuts to mothers-in-law, horses were hit with hammers, cousins punched cousins and nuns fisted priests. It was a sad and disastrous time in Irish history and, probably most tragically of all, the only thing we were really left with at the end of it all was Fianna Fáil and Fine Gael.

Catholic Ireland

After independence, the Irish were exhausted from fighting and unsure about what to do with their freedom, so they handed the keys of the country to the bishops and went to the pub. In those early years, Ireland was run as a sort of dreary outpost of the Vatican by an emotionally retarded patriarchy, supervised by Archbishop John Charles McQuaid, who observed the nation from a giant marble pulpit erected across the Dublin skyline. From his pulpit, McQuaid would sit tutting and pontificating, occasionally swooping down on courting couples, ensuring their hips were kept well separated and their minds pure and innocent. He would send out Christian Brothers like those winged monkeys from *The Wizard of Oz*, to supernaturally enter into the horny dreams of teenagers, replacing their indecent fantasies with visions of Padre Pio randomly curing things. In order to keep the country in this state of suspended grace, the government began an extensive campaign of censorship, banning everything in sight – books, films, jazz, the Second World War, Sophia Loren, French pen pals, the colour blue, the letter X, loose sheep . . . In truth, nothing was safe.

Soon, a strict social hierarchy began to emerge.

Ireland in Europe

In 1973, after about fifty uninterrupted years of polio and confession, Ireland joined the EEC. This was as a direct result of Dana winning the Eurovision three years earlier. Although primarily done to annoy the United Kingdom, it soon began to pay off. Structural funds flowed. Common Agricultural Policy money swilled. There were lakes of wine to drink and mountains of butter to slap on our brown bread. Finally, things were beginning to look up! Ireland could throw off the shackles of imperial and religious oppression and build for the future, as Europe began to drag us kicking and screaming out of the fifteenth century. The croissant was introduced, roads were built, a family in Drogheda broke loose by not having their dinner in the middle of the day ... Suddenly, the whole place became obsessed with education – by the 1990s a whole generation had been packed off to university to learn about the law, macroeconomics, pharmaceuticals (the preparation and ingestion thereof) and The Pixies. Everything was primed for an economic revolution. When it came ... oh my good God Jesus Christ Almighty And All The Saints Preserve Us When I Think About It did it come.

The Celtic Tiger

Like many people of my generation, I often have terrible anxiety dreams that the Celtic Tiger has returned again and I wake up with a start, completely drenched in champagne. It is difficult to explain this period to the younger generation of today – I always think of it as a cross between a Roman vomitorium and the scene in *Charlie and the Chocolate Factory* where Augustus Gloop swims around in the chocolate river, but even that doesn't quite do it justice.

The streets of Dublin glistened white with a light dusting of half-consumed cocaine that hugged the footpaths. Celtic Women, as they were by then known, spent their evenings draped lithely over generous kitchen islands licking toffee-covered strawberries while their husbands circled the room on Segways quaffing more Prosecco from the gleaming Smeg fridge. Property prices were rising so fast in Dublin that you could actually hear the sound of sizzling when you stuck your head out the window. Indeed, *The Irish Times* property section became so bloated and unwieldy, one unlucky delivery-man had to be rescued by the fire brigade after falling into it. Meanwhile, Bertie Ahern held sway across the land, swanning around the place like Del Boy after he strikes it rich, while Charlie McCreevy sprayed borrowed money around like it was organic fertilizer.

It was absolutely disgusting.

What many people don't know is that it all started off in a most humble way. In the late nineties a man called Willie in Cavan found five Irish punts down the back of his couch. He went on to place this money on a horse called Serendipity, running in the 3.30 at Cheltenham, at odds of 20/1. The horse won and Willie embarked on a winning streak, which was to last for six months and over which time he managed to build up a fund of £1,247. On 1 January 2002, this magically turned into €1508.87 in the new currency, the euro. Like many Irish people, Willie thought he became 21 per cent richer overnight and began to spend money like a fiend. Using his €1,500, Willie borrowed €250,000 from an Irish bank who themselves borrowed it from a German pensioner called Klaus, who hadn't a clue what Willie was up to. Willie invested this money in a three-bedroomed house in Cootehill. After a week, the bank phoned Willie to offer him another three hundred thousand euros if he released the equity in his current home and bought a buy-to-let apartment. Willie said 'Keeeee-yaavan' (he accepted) and thus started an economic miracle, whereby thousands of Willies around Ireland bought and sold property to one another, creating a housing bubble so large it could eventually be seen from space.

Hey, we all partied. *All* of us. Many people pretend they didn't. A man from Longford famously appeared on *Prime Time* to explain how he was still waiting for *his* Celtic Tiger, how it had passed him by, but sure enough, three weeks later, photos emerged of him in Las Vegas the previous summer, up to his waist in chocolate and hookers, as he casually petted a puma. He left Ireland the next day, disgraced and alone, his head bowed in shame as he boarded the plane to Ibiza.

The Bank Guarantee

Unfortunately, Klaus wanted his money back. The end had to come. And oh my good God Jesus Christ Almighty And All The Saints Preserve Us When I Think About It did it come.

In 2008, after the collapse of Lehman Brothers, Brian Cowen's government was shocked to discover that the house of cards on which the whole Irish economic 'miracle' was based was actually stacked upon another house of cards, a far flimsier construction that was held together using chewing gum and Pritt Stick, and which itself was balanced precariously on four other separate houses of cards, each one more badly constructed than the other, all of which was balanced on the edge of a cliff over a sea full of sharks that ate houses of cards for breakfast.

It was a terrifying vista.

It's not that the emperor didn't have any clothes, it's that the emperor wasn't even really an emperor at all, he was actually the guy who cut the emperor's grass and he was parading around as this naked emperor, while everybody else looked on presuming he had completely lost it.

To pull out of this economic nosedive, a unilateral display of strength was required, a stroke of such terrifying Fianna Fáilness, that everyone in Ireland woke up paralysed down the left side the morning after it happened. This stroke – the bank guarantee – was the stroke to beat all strokes and involved guaranteeing the debts of Ireland's shittiest banks (basically all of them) with the people's money (basically all of it), the nation state equivalent of acting as guarantor on the mortgages of an entire graduating class from a clown school.

The economy imploded. The sky fell in. Brian Cowen ran away to hide with Bertie in the bushes. The Troika arrived to the opening chords of 'Ride of the Valkyries'.

All of a sudden, we were where we were.

Revisionism: What Might Have Been

But did it need to turn out thus? Could anything have been done to change the trajectory? To prevent Ireland going boom and bust, boom and bust? Before we move on with the rest of this guide, it's worth considering for a moment some other permutations, how things might have been.

1. What if Michael Collins Had Been a Dwarf?

Collins's nickname, 'The Big Fella', suggested a sort of big-brotherly manliness. It exuded power, implying a steady hand and strong leadership. But what if Collins had been a man of smaller stature, say a dwarf? Would his rise to prominence in the republican movement have been thwarted by prejudice? Would it have made him dangerously insecure, like Adolf Hitler? Might Lloyd George have sat on him by mistake? What then for the British Empire? Or would his assassin in Béal na mBláth simply have missed by a few inches?

2. What if Countess Markievicz Had Been a Man?

Constance Markievicz was the first woman in the world to hold a Cabinet position. However, if she had been born with male genitals, might she instead have become Count Markievicz, the first vampire in the world to hold a Cabinet position? Would this have strengthened our hand against the British, having an immortal creature of the night on our negotiating team? Would the Dáil have had to sit in darkness in order to accomodate his vulnerability to sunlight? Could Ireland have become the best little country in the world in which to drink blood? How would this have affected the culture? Would you happily line out against a vampire in a camogie match? Would you sit in front of one at an Omniplex?

3. What if the English Had Been Sound?

What if Oliver Cromwell had been really dead on, say like Michael Palin? What if instead of rampaging through the coun-tryside, setting our fields on fire and murdering our horses, he had gently trotted into town, doing one-liners, performing surreal sketches and recounting tales of his travels throughout the Empire? Would there have been such hostility and subsequent bloodshed? Would *The Graham Norton Show* now be shot in Bandon? Would the 'Irish Breakfast' even exist as a food movement?

4. What if de Valera Had Gotten the Ride?

It must have pained de Valera to see Michael Collins swanning around Dublin on his High Nelly, cracking jokes, driving Kitty O'Shea wild. The Big Fella really was the Justin Timberlake of the international anti-colonial independence movement. But what would Dev have been like as a leader if fate had dealt him a different hand? What if he had enjoyed a steamy, all-night threesome across in America? Would 'comely maidens dancing at the crossroads' have been replaced by gritty, burlesque cabaret clubs? Would the simple shawl have been renounced in favour of leather tank tops and nipple clamps? Would Ireland have been less a repressed, priest-ridden backwater and more an Ibiza-style rave destination? Would he ever have gone blind?

4. What if Charles J. Haughey Had Been Honest?

If Charlie had been honest he would have survived for about five minutes in Fianna Fáil at the time. This would have necessitated him searching for work elsewhere. Could his love of fancy shirts have led him into a career as a tailor, perhaps? Might he have therefore travelled to Paris to learn his trade at Charvet Place Vendôme, crafting bespoke pyjamas for French aristocrats and happily gorging on ortolan? Might he have then returned to Ireland a major international success, to get a gig dressing Taoisigh Dessie O'Malley or Mary Harney? Would Bertie Ahern ever have gone into politics or would he have ended up running a greyhound stadium instead? Would any of us have had to tighten our belts? How many millions would we have saved on tribunals?

Chapter 5

Town and Country

Map of
IRELAND

Wild Atlantic
Way

Shergar

Giant's
Causeway

Boy
Racers

Puke
Football

Place
Conveniently
Not Covered
In This
Book

Chicargo

Not
WB Yeats

Possibly
Fermanagh

More
Artists

Area
51

Fuck Off
Shell

Artists

Cyavan

Steve
Staunton

Sellafield

Hardy
Bucks

Ming's
Planet
Mongo

Con
Shine's
Lobby

Multiple
'Meaths'

Dublin City
('Administrative
Capital)

TG4

Galway City

BIFFOs

Deaf
Soldiers

Birthplace of
Mary Coughlan

Avoca

Cliffs! Lots of Cliffs!!

Fiddlers

The Demesne
Of Lowry

Kilkenny
'City'

Carlow

Boy
Racers

Limerick

Guards

Berlin

Boy
Racers

Buttevant

Wawherford

Mechanical
Dolphin
Zone

Yanks

Gift of
the glob

The Sunny
South East

Black Pudding

Cork City
(Spiritual Capital)

City Life

Although **Ireland** is probably best known worldwide as a green pastoral land, filled with farmhands writing poetry and dirty-faced children gawping out of black-and-white photos, we also have cities and towns and electricity and restaurants and Netflix and lots of other stuff misty-eyed Irish Americans would probably prefer never to know about. Michael Fassbender is from Kerry.

So, as well as the twee villages with the people mostly made of wool and the women in the B&Bs who have been sculpted entirely out of Kerrygold, there are some pretty hip metropolitan zones in Ireland, towns and cities where the young converge and the old are being slowly forced out with selfie sticks.

Here is some basic information that you'll need in order to survive the main Irish conurbations.

Cork

Sitting picturesquely on the banks of their own lovely Lee, Cork is the second-biggest city in the Republic of Ireland and is often referred to as 'the real capital', exclusively by the people who live there.

Unfortunately, it is not the capital city. It also isn't a

people's republic. It's got an English Market, for fuck's sake.

Despite the fact that Cork has been awarded TripAdvisor's City with the Highest Self-esteem Award for four years running, Corkonians do tend to suffer from a sort of second-city syndrome, a unique cocktail of profound arrogance and horrifying insecurity. Sometimes the form do be bad, like.

Corkonians love Cork with an almost religious fervour, but despite a generally cheerful, good-natured outlook, they are also prone to turning on one another from time to time and even snapping at strangers, in the very same way beautiful dogs sometimes maul children because of prolonged maltreatment at the hands of a previous owner.

Cork people who live outside Cork are notorious for their obsession with Cork. It is almost impossible to engage in conversation with a Cork exile without the subject of Cork coming up repeatedly as that Cork person goes on and on in that Cork way of theirs, namechecking Cork again and again and again and again and reminiscing about the pure, unending Corkness of it all, boy, and how they're planning on moving back home soon and out of this godforsaken kip (Dublin). And sure they'll be back home doin' Pana in their rubber dollies suppin' Tanora in no time, like.

Galway

Galway is a gorgeous, bustling city on the west coast of Ireland, with all the local charm of a small farming village and sometimes the personal hygiene to match. It is not well understood but for some reason about 95 per cent of the population of Galway is employed making puppets with big weird heads on them.

Many Galway people come from a long genetic line that

runs all the way back to the Spanish Armada. This explains their often sallow complexions and dark curly hair, not to mention their mysteriously deep affection for overpriced tapas. Often referred to by other Irish people as hippies or crusties, this is a patently unfair stereotype, completely betraying the wide diversity of the city.

As well as hippies and crusties, Galwegians now also count among their number jugglers, traditional fiddlers, circus midgets, bearded ladies, spoon-playing tramps, wankers on stilts and Gaeilgeoirí, as well as a whole subculture of people who will blow smoke out their hoops for a fiver.

Kilkenny

A stunningly beautiful town nestled on the banks of the River Nore, Kilkenny gains its city status because it has its own cathedral. In truth, Kilkenny is only a city in the way my grandmother's coalshed is the International Space Station. And with a population of about eight thousand, Kilkenny can piss off if it thinks it's getting a proper section in this book.

Dublin

Dublin is a thriving European capital, split down the middle by the River Liffey, which was dug out of the land and filled with green sludge by Liam Lawlor in the late 1990s to keep poor people out of the Southside.

Previously a smog-filled shitbox riddled with tenements and coddle, for years many Dubliners were poor and destitute, a vast cohort of them spending much of the 1960s living in Ronnie Drew's beard.

But Dublin has transformed in recent years and is now one

of the great hipster meccas of Europe. Indeed, it is going head-to-head with places like Berlin and Lisbon, where the growing wealth of the populace can easily be gauged by the levels of oversubscribed Sunday brunch and pricks carrying vinyl. Whereas in the past the phrase 'pulled pork' might only have been used in Ireland to describe shifting a garda, nowadays it is the food filling of choice for a generation of young Irish, who spend much of their time consuming and consuming and consuming in a pointless effort to postpone the reality of their inevitable deaths, which approaches them all, regardless, clawing at them with its icy fingers.

Or at least that's the impression I get when I see them ordering frozen yoghurt on Wexford Street.

In recent times, the influx of tech companies like Google, Facebook and Yahoo! has confirmed Dublin's reputation as a European tech capital. Indeed, it is hoped that by the year 2024, up to 80 per cent of Dublin could exist entirely on the Internet. This may be the only realistic solution to the city's housing crisis, where the architectural equivalent of an outside toilet will still sell for north of five hundred thousand euros. Unfortunately, this problem isn't going away. The population of Ireland is amassing on the east coast at such a worrying rate that some experts believe the entire country could become lopsided and flip over sideways on to Wales by the year 2050. This could be catastrophic for Anglo-Irish relations, not to mention the car-ferry industry. At this stage, town planners are pinning all their hopes on the possibility that broadband technology develops to such a degree that future Dubs could be uploaded to the cloud and that the homeless might simply be deleted altogether.

Wawherford

Blaa, blaa.

Limerick

Known affectionately throughout Ireland as Stab City, due to the high rate of knife crimes there in past decades, Limerick really has much more to offer than random blade attacks. Contrary to the lazy stereotype, Limerick also has its fair share of shootings, punishment beatings, whippings, tiger kidnappings and even occasional scaldings to add to its repertoire. To mix it up, they sometimes drop pianos on people.

But it's not all bad. Limerick is also home to Munster Rugby, whose never-say-die attitude is so legendary they've stopped planning for graveyards. Limerick also boasts some particularly stunning Georgian architecture, a castle and the Shannon, voted Ireland's sexiest river in a recent TV3 primetime series called *Ireland's Sexiest Rivers*.

It's worth mentioning, however, that whoever wrote the song 'Limerick, You're A Lady' probably never went out to Ballinacurra Weston to buy a ten-spot.

The Country

Country people, or 'culchies' – the name to which they are often reduced – are a lot like hobbits. They are carefree, quick to friendship, loyal to a fault and many of them possess outsized hairy feet, particularly the women.

Without Irish country people there would be no GAA or hang sangwiches, no *Up for the Match* or peat briquettes, no Jackie Healy-Rae or lengths of Wavin pipe. Without them, there would be no strawberries for sale at the side of the road, no foot-and-mouth disease and you could forget about ever seeing those big 'Best of luck, Mary!' banners in the studio audience for *Winning Streak*.

There would also be no studio audience for *Winning Streak*.

To really understand rural Ireland, you have to understand a little bit about community. We all know this from SuperValu adverts and Things That Marty Morrissey Says, but it's worth remembering. The Irish word *meitheal* describes an old custom where country people would gather together as a community to help save the hay on a neighbour's farm. (It is not to be confused with *heavy meitheal*, which describes the mysterious obsession country people have with AC/DC). You see this sense of community in organizations like Macra na Feirme and TidyTowns, where people volunteer their time for the good of the parish, taking pride in their own place and doing everything within their power to beat those fuckers in the next parish over. You see it in the straggling lines outside a funeral home where people are only going to 'show their face'. Indeed, coming from a small Irish parish is a bit of a lifetime commitment. Locals will always wonder about what you are doing and they are delighted to welcome you home with a gentle, warm embrace. The bonds are strong.

In many ways, it would be easier to get away from a particularly obsessed branch of Scientologists.

Country people, wherever they are, bring this love of parish with them. Indeed they will often form mini-communities within minutes. This is best observed when you see folk from different parts of Ireland meeting for the first time. Initially it is like watching nervous dogs – circling around, sizing each other up and sniffing each other's arses, etc. But once friendship and trust is established, they'll be off running in a pack, playing, chasing cats, drinking red lemonade, shitting in gardens, etc. Country people have their own unique shorthand and code when they are together (officially called English), something 'city folk' like Bill Cullen and Kim Kardashian will simply never fully understand.

The Sky at Night

One of the best ways to experience the country is alone, in the dark. *(It may help to read the following section in the voice of an old sailor, reminiscing.)*

Picture it. You're in a country pub in the middle of West Kerry. You've had a pint. You've had another pint. You've had a drop of whiskey for the road. You've had one last pint, no messing like, we'll definitely row for the shore, then . . . Mikey Daly stands you another pint and you're all 'Feck it, go on', before knocking it back and making your excuses.

As you stumble out into the darkness and move away from the dull hubbub of the bar, something hits you, something that people from large conurbations like Dusseldorf and, say, Mallow have to experience to really believe.

The silence of the Irish countryside.

For it is surely one of the loudest sounds in the universe.

In days gone by you might have been able to jump on the back of an old horse and cart and shout 'Home' to the waiting animal. Or you might have crawled into the driver's seat of a Ford Cortina to zigzag your way home through the gardens and fields, accumulating a small farmyard of livestock, briars and assorted tillage on your front bumper as you drunk-drove.

Sensibly, these days you must walk. Using your limbs, nervous system and the small part of your brain left after the night's libations.

This country silence seems more intense on a clear, starry night. As you step along the lonely boreen, asphalt illuminated by the moon, briars clawing at you from hedgerows as if to make conversation, you almost tiptoe along. It feels that if you didn't, you might wake some sleeping, invisible giant, probably called Feidhelm, and he might rise up high into the sky – bungalows hanging out of him and cows plummeting into the sea – and march off into the darkness.

Sure, there are occasions when the purr of a distant taxi or the forlorn bray of a lonely donkey will kill the ambience. But the silence, when it descends again, like some sort of surreal sonic dishcloth, is one of the wonders of the Irish countryside. You hear your heart thumping in your chest – ta-dum, ta-dum, ta-dum – the blood pumping around your head – sswwwws- ssshhhhhhhhhhh – listen hard and you can just about hear your own fingernails growing.

On clear nights like this, as you amble along and turn your gaze upwards, the constellations of the night sky seem almost uncomfortably close. It's like Orion the Hunter could unpin himself from the cosmos, climb down along Ursa Minor and cartwheel off across the fields with Feidhelm. You could almost grab the Plough with your hands and fling it off into the Atlantic. It's not just that you might be staring into the face of God but that He is standing right up against you, touching your nose with His, breathing heavily into your cheeks, like an angry Roy Keane in the tunnel of a stadium. On nights like this, on the outer edges of Europe, you feel so at one with the universe, it's actually kind of awkward.

Well, either that or it's the booze.

It's little wonder that over the centuries, assorted waifs and drunken vagabonds – their livers swollen with poitín, their brains on fire with magic mushrooms – would imagine the most bizarre things on these strange midnight rambles. Leprechauns and faeries, headless horsemen and banshees, UFOs and unexpected Garda checkpoints . . .

Grand spot all the same.

Culchies in Dublin

Many culchies disappear into Dublin, usually around the college years, and simply forget to go home. Drawn into the city by the bright lights, the big noise and Copper Face Jacks, this silent mass is all around and they can be hard to spot to the untrained eye. (Apart from GAA weekends, when they literally couldn't be easier to spot.)

You can often see them standing around looking wistfully at Other Places postboxes or leafing sadly through the sports sections of regional newspapers. Stroll past any pub window and they can be observed, drinking alone, staring into the void, fantasizing about tractors, probably.

Although these people fit in well enough, it's easy to forget that they are also very different to their Dublin brethren. They have a completely different sense of humour, for a start. In Dublin 'Piss off home ya bollix' might be considered playful banter or a cheeky way to say goodbye to your mother-in-law, but this would be an aggressive tone to take with a country person. Country humour is more inclusive. We might gather at a gate to laugh at horses, for example. Or we might enjoy the aul' craic by, for example, setting an old Protestant house on fire.

Going home is always in the back of our minds though and where Cork people are concerned, this is often painfully apparent.

Rebels with a Cause

Rebel 1: *Were you at the All-Ireland?*

Rebel 2: *Septic.*

R1: *The hurlers wouldn't let us down like that.*

R2: *Would they fuck. You can always depend on the hurlers. Were you down home recently?*

R1: *Was yeah, last night.*

R2: *On a Tuesday?*

R1: *Arrah, I was lonesome. Went down to Hillbilly's for a burger around nine and drove back up again this morning. I was at my desk by around five ta.*

R2: *Daycent! Will you ever move back, ja think?*

R1: *Oh, chalk it down boy. I'd be back in the morning if it wasn't for herself. You?*

R2: *Ah yeah. Just need to save up enough.*

R1: *Tell me about it.*

R2: *Once I get my shit together, I'll be off sooner than you can say 'There are delays on approach at the Jack Lynch Tunnel'.*

R2: *'Tis a fine tunnel.*

R1: *De best a dem. Better than the Port Tunnel anyway.*

R2: *C'mere to me, your wife's a Dub yeah?*

R1: *She is. Why?*

R2: *How wouldja deal? Having jackeen spawn?*

R1: *It's a problem, pal. I won't lie to you.*

R2: *'Magine them coming up to ya – 'Hoooowya Daaaaa, wouldja giz a few quid for Doctor Quiiiiiirrrrrrkeeey's?'*

R1: *Jesus Christ, I know . . .*

R2: *'Will yiz join us on The Hill, Daaaaa? Fur the Duuuubbbbillllinn gay-am.'*

R1: *Here, that's not funny. Christ . . .*

R2: *'The bleedin' cuuuuuuulchies have to sit dowan at the backarra bus, Daaaa.'*

R1: *Ah here, I'm away off. You're annoying me now.*

R2: *I'm only hoppin' the ball. See ya later on ya gimp.*

R2: *Langer.*

Contemporary Civil Wars

In Ireland, even after nearly a century of independence, there is a phenomenon whereby we all begin to fidget and get a bit antsy with each other every couple of summers.

For some reason, every now and then, IRELAND NEEDS A CIVIL WAR.

WARNING: We are now travelling to the very heart of the Irish psyche. It would be advisable to wear goggles and leave your sense of proportion at the door.

The basic subtext to all these national crises is as follows. On one side, country people think Dublin people are patronizing them somehow and causing them a great slight. On the other side, the D4 chattering classes can't help sneering at the great unwashed beyond the M50.

Let me give you a few examples.

In 2014, 'Garthgate' rocked Ireland to its very core when the singer Garth Brooks was refused planning permission to play five nights in a row in Croke Park, unfortunately after the tickets had already sold out.

The media went bananas. Grown men were found crying in the streets. Forlorn women from rural Limerick marched on the Dáil, threatening to set their Stetsons on fire. Guilty grandparents tried to explain to grandchildren why Mammy and Daddy had set a giant wicker effigy of Owen Keegan, chief executive of Dublin City Council, on fire on the back lawn. *Liveline* went into the stratosphere, creating a visible vortex of outrage over Ireland.

What began as a small scuffle (a local planning dispute) escalated into a bitter war (carefully orchestrated media strategies on all sides), which ultimately divided the nation, leaving us completely disgraced the world over (the global media smirked for about five minutes), with our international reputation in tatters (seriously, none of them actually gave a rat's arse) and our future as a sovereign nation on the brink of collapse (well, this was actually true but for other resaons, outlined earlier). It was typical of a silly-season storm in Ireland. But why does this happen?

It could be all the pent-up nervous energy that builds over

many months of being overly polite to each other. Maybe we just need a good fight? Anyone in a relationship knows that sometimes you have to have a massive and pointless argument over curtains just to clear the air. Whatever the deep-seated reasons, past scandals like these are just too numerous to list, but include incidents like the civil war over Saipan, GUBU, the Hand of Henry, the street riots over the cancellation of *Glenroe* and the tragic series of hunger strikes that took place in response to Marty Whelan deciding not to dye his hair any more.

Here are the basic ingredients for a national scandal:

1   A national schism divided along rural and urban lines.

2   A Jesus-like protagonist who can act as hero or villain depending on your side in the civil war, e.g. Roy Keane, Garth Brooks.

3   A controversial authority figure who can act as hero or villain depending on your side in the civil war, e.g. Mick McCarthy, Owen Keegan.

4   A government who are more than happy with this timely distraction, given the absolute state of the place, and who promise to intervene in a shamelessly populist pursuit of votes, e.g. Bertie Ahern stopping just short of offering to wash Roy Keane's feet when he arrived home from Saipan.

5   A national media that is a bit bored in the middle of summer.

6   An Irish public who badly need to let off a bit of steam, God help them.

7   A developing sense of national shame and embarrassment that the world is looking on, when the world media
clearly isn't.

8   A number of successive days of extended recrimination,
manic appeals, unseemly spats and a general atmosphere of
frenzy expertly overseen by Joe Duffy and the rest of the
Liveline team.

Chapter 6

Food

The early Irish, being hunter-gatherers, enjoyed a fairly lean diet of nuts, berries and the very occasional mammoth. By all accounts they were slim, lithe and fantastically sexy human beings – a million miles away from the thunderous blubber-butts of today.

Things started to go badly wrong around the time Sir Walter Raleigh introduced the humble spud on his vast estate in Youghal in the 1580s. Now this fella had form. He seemed intent on ruining the long-term health of Europeans. Not only did he bring potatoes from the Americas to fatten us up, he brought back tobacco to destroy everyone's lungs, cheese burritos to clog up our arteries and the twelve-speed racer to fuck up our knees.

As we know, the Irish became very dependent on the potato, so much so that by the year 1832 it is believed 92 per cent of the native population survived on cheese-and-onion crisps alone. The inevitable result of all this was the failure of the potato crop and consequently the Great Famine. The Irish developed a complex, often uneasy attitude towards food and eating, an attitude neatly summed up by the phrase 'Will ya ever ate it!'

The 'Will ya ever ate it!' approach to dining basically involves stuffing your face with every available foodstuff in sight. Traditionally, food was not savoured for its texture or flavour, or indeed discussed ad nauseam across kitchen islands in Dalkey by people called Muirgheal. Food was a thing to be grabbed and quickly hidden away in your stomach in case somebody English got their hands on it. A remnant of 'Will ya ever ate it!' can still be observed today at Sunday carveries across the land, as families set about the task of completely ignoring one another while hoovering up food like they're Hungry Hippos with the munchies. There is a wild abandon about the way we eat sometimes, a sort of rabid intensity, perhaps betraying a subconscious fear that Oliver Cromwell is going to appear in our peripheral vision and whip the plate out from under us.

Modern attitudes to food in Ireland are changing, however. It's fair to say that restaurant culture, food standards and people's palates have advanced remarkably since the 1990s. It's less 'Will ya ever ate it!' and more 'Would ya ever pass us the jalapeños there, Seamus?' and we have the Italians to thank for two pivotal turning points along the way.

The Eye-talian Chipper

The Italians are internationally renowned as prime exponents of superb cuisine and this proud epicurean culture has developed slowly since antiquity. Family recipes are passed down through the generations, utilizing a wide range of delicious fresh vegetables, herbs and spices to make delectable tomato sauces and exquisitely cooked meat, fish and vegetarian dishes. It may come as some surprise, then, that they came all the way to Ireland to introduce the battered sausage and curry chip.

But Italian chippers opened Irish eyes to the wonders of fast food by performing a sort of coronary invasion of the country that still proudly survives to this day. Before we knew it, we were a takeaway nation, converging on chippers like locusts or else slowly arching our necks around doorways to quickly grab paper bags from men on motorbikes, hoping the neighbours don't see us embark on another shameful evening of gluttony, sloth and bad television.

The Day the Pasta Came

Just as many older people can remember exactly where they were the day JFK was assassinated, the same can be said for The Day the Pasta Came in the late 1980s. Confusion reigned for the first while. Many supermarket owners mistakenly stocked pasta in the gardening section as fertilizer. Children would play with it on the street like tiddlywinks. I know of at least one woman who wore rigatoni earrings to Mass. When pasta was finally revealed to be for human consumption (probably in a state-of-the-nation intervention by Gay Byrne), households would often purchase it out of curiosity before gathering in the kitchen to nervously poke at it like apes round a monolith. Inevitably, it would sit there for months – usually on a shelf with an unopened bottle of lemon juice and an out-of-date packet of Chivers jelly – until a curious soul would one day bravely boil it up, before eating it straight from the pot without any sauce.

Modern and Traditional

Nowadays, things couldn't be more different. Ireland is punching well above its weight on the international food scene. We've signed cheese and butter deals with the Chinese government, committing to make all Chinese people fat by the year 2050 and we're actually producing enough Irish cheese to keep the rest of Europe in nightmares for the foreseeable future. Indeed, there are so many new and interesting restaurants of outstanding quality opening up all around the country, you'd nearly have a heart attack just thinking about it. There's a veritable smorgasbord of actual smorgasbords for us all to enjoy.

But in order to understand our current obsession with food, it's vital to look back into the past, to our traditional dishes, as it might be time to rediscover some of the culinary fare unique to this little island.

Traditional Irish Boxty

Boxty is a traditional Irish potato pancake. The word 'boxty' comes from the Irish *arán bocht tí*, meaning 'poorhouse bread', which is hardly the best sales pitch. Boxty, like much Irish food, is taking off again in the hipster restaurants of Ireland's cities where a sort of culinary upcycling is beginning to take place, essentially repackaging cheap stuff in steampunk clothes to sell at exorbitant prices to the growing hordes of hungry German software engineers.

Ingredients
250g old spuds • 250g new spuds • 250g mashed spuds • 250g roast spuds • 250g garlic spuds • 250g spuds • 250g flour • 1 tsp salt • 1 tsp baking powder • lump of butter the size of your fisht • bottle of milk

1 Fuck all the ingredients into a box and shake vigorously.

2 Fuck the food on to a plate.

3 Ate it!

Traditional Dublin Coddle

Coddle is a traditional dish designed to use up leftovers and is another big hit with the hipsters, even if hipster leftovers generally include pulled pork, acres of kale and kangaroo steaks. The original Dublin version is a much simpler proposition and is guaranteed to warm the cockles/muscles/your colon.

Ingredients
1 packet a rashers • 1 Oxo cube • 1 pair a Darndale socks • 1 packet a sausos • 6 spuds • 2 onions • a glugga de gargle • salt and pepper • 1 sprig a Ronnie Drew's whiskers

1 Hack the rashers up in strips using a blunt Stanley blade and boil up your stock along with your freshly removed, week-old Darndale socks.

2 Heap in the sausos and the rashers and boil the living shit out of them. After around three hummed choruses of 'McAlpine's Fusiliers', pour off and save the stock, then fire in the veggies from an excitable distance.

3 Cook for as long as it takes to walk from the junction at Summerhill to Ned's of Townsend Street.

4 Add the stock and a glugga de gargle and then simmer for around fifteen peals of St Peter's Church bells, Phibsborough.

5 Season then garnish with a sprig of Ronnie Drew's whiskers and serve in an aul' uptoorned ha'.

Traditional Dingle Chowder

Adored by fishermen and tourists alike, this dish is particularly comforting on a wet winter's day next to a warm, crackling fire in the corner of a pub, ideally with an Irish wolfhound curled at your tired and aching feet. Alternatively, you can pick up a carton in Tesco fairly cheap.

Ingredients
25g butter • onion • leek • carrot • spud • 120ml rank Irish white wine • thingamajig of fish stock • 4 deveined Dublin Bay prawns pummelled with an ESB pole • 25g John Dory • 1 langerload of pollock • 50g desiccated sturgeon's hoop • 50g flatfish • 50g monkfish • 1 quart of Fungi the Dolphin's tears • 350mg of the steam off a GAA All Star's piss • far, far, FAR too much cream • 250g Wren Boy eyelashes (toasted) • 1 pack of Buffalo Hunky Dorys

1 Heat a large pan and fire in the butter and veg. Sauté for a few minutes before pouring in the disgusting Irish white wine, hoping/praying that it quickly reduces by half before it destroys everything.

2 Add the fish stock, pummelled prawns, John Dory, pollock, desiccated sturgeon hoop and other assorted fish and then spatter liberally with the freshly harvested tears of Fungi using a small plastic holy-water dispenser.

3 Cover and steam over a boiling pot of (preferably) a GAA All Star's urine before horsing in 'enough cream to close a road'.

4 Simmer for an aeon before garnishing with the toasted eyelashes of last year's Wren Boys.

5 Crumble over the Buffalo Hunky Dorys and serve with homemade brown bread, obviously.

Traditional Irish Box Player

There's an infamous pub in East Clare favoured by traditional musicians for its fine pub grub. What many of these musicians don't realize is that a large number of accordion players have disappeared, having gone to the jacks during a break from the music. It seems these box players are sluiced through a secret trapdoor into an underground slaughterhouse where they are minced and diced in jig time, before being baked slowly in a pie and served to their unwitting but ravenous colleagues. Some of the other musicians have become suspicious of the mournful drones emanating from the otherwise delicious pies. Otherwise, their disappearance has not been noticed.

Hang Sangwiches

Hang was first imported to Ireland by the Chinese Hang Dynasty in AD 137 and it's fair to say we haven't looked back since. Hang is harvested from the meat of pigs after which it is customarily rolled into gigantic forty-foot oval bales, a task often performed by up to forty strapping men using railway sleepers. These oozing, dripping bales of raw meat are then stored deep underground in Hang Caves, thousands of miles of which stretch underneath Cavan, also known as the Hang Belt. These dark, porous, limestone caverns offer the perfect growing conditions for the hang, where it can stay moist and cool and where it is slowly age-flavoured by the droppings of bats. Hang bales are often skewered in place using stalagmites and can be stored underground for up to twenty years until such time as they come to taste 'hangsome'. This can only be ascertained by a crack team of expert tasters, known as hangmen, who practise an artisan craft that has been passed on through the generations. At the end of this process, the hang will be cut up and delivered in batches to butchers, where you can order it by the slice. The live ball of hang will often be cut in front of you with a frightening machine called a hangsaw, which would 'take the hand off you' if you weren't careful.

Hang sangwiches – by far the best delivery system for the hang to reach the digestive system – can be made by almost anyone, following this very simple recipe.

Ingredients
• *2 slices of plain white bread* •*Your own body weight in pure Irish butter* • *2–3 slices of delicious hang*

1 Take both slices of white bread and layer generously with butter (a shitload is recommended).

2 Press 2 to 3 slices of hang (simple, basic, honest-to-God hang please) into this butter mountain and depress with great determination (sticking out your tongue helps!). It is best to wear an apron so as to avoid flying, rogue spurts of butter.

3 Once the hang has been secured, place the second slice of bread on top firmly.

4 Ensure the hang is 'locked in' by sitting on the sangwich for as little as 5 minutes in a warm armchair.

5 Serve on a small plate with a side bag of Tayto and a cup of tae, or simply keep in cling film or tin foil for later consumption, e.g. during half-time at the match.

WARNING: Overconsumption of hang results in a condition known as hang brain – a confused, muddled, often terrifying state. Hang brain can be observed in the gawping, confounded faces of suited, elderly men sitting in parked cars for hours on a

Sunday afternoon. Many of these individuals will most likely be coming down from a gluttonous episode involving copious Sunday hang and they often wear an expression not unlike that of the figure in Edvard Munch's *The Scream*. It goes without saying that these individuals should not be approached under any circumstances.

Tae

In the film *Amélie* the protagonist famously stood overlooking the Parisian skyline imagining all the French people having sex in the city below. You can do the exact same thing overlooking Dublin, if you imagine all the people drinking tae.

During Penal times, the native Irish risked life and limb to secretly gather around rocks in the middle of fields to drink Irish tae. Nowadays, thanks to great strides in the field of human rights, Irish people are free to drink tae with wild abandon. Indeed, consumption has reached such dizzying peaks that it is thought the average Irish person, randomly pricked with a knitting needle, would spurt out enough tae to fill a Belfast sink.

The truth is, there's no amount of tension that the phrases 'Sure, I'll put on the kettle' or 'You'll have a cup in the hand?' can't immediately dissolve – the break up of a marriage, losing your job, even a domestic homicide. So it makes sense to have a pot or a couple of bags on your person at all times.

Note: Like many things in Ireland, the enjoyment of tae is still divided along civil-war lines, so it is smart to know whether you are in a Barry's or Lyons area before scalding the pot.

Bacon and Cabbage

Bacon and cabbage is a popular traditional Irish meal, as nutritious as it is tasty, and it is usually accompanied by a fairly unforgettable smell. Indeed, the honk off bacon and cabbage can pervade a house with almost supernatural intensity, clinging to the walls and the unlucky inhabitants for days. The signature bang of bacon and cabbage has even been known to settle on a village like mist, creating a noxious tropical microclimate, which fogs up kitchen windows, corrodes the insides of car engines and causes cattle to go loopy. Luckily, the stench can easily be combatted if the locals can muster up enough brown sauce between them as a sort of perfume antidote. This can be done by leaving buckets of brown sauce out on the lawn overnight, rubbing brown sauce all over their bodies (especially the armpits and groins), or by simply spraying the town in a brown-sauce vapour using e.g. a Garda helicopter.

I've decided against including the recipe for bacon and cabbage here to avoid stinking up the rest of the book.

Chapter 7

The Drink

A recent **World** Health Organization survey of Irish attitudes to drinking was found crumpled up in a canal, covered in Guinness stains and the WHO official was located three
days later having married a yoga instructor from Kilkee by
mistake.

After the Estonians, the Austrians and the French (who
have a blood-alcohol limit that it is illegal to be under), we are,
per capita, up there with the best of them in the field of alcoholic self-abuse. If you stick your head out the window on any
given Sunday morning, you can hear the phrase 'I'm never
drinking again' roll across the hills like birdsong.

We have a bit of a problem.

In France, they'll slowly sip wine with their breakfast,
brunch, lunch, dinner and supper. In Ireland, when it's time to
drink, we commit to it entirely. A meal is seen as a waste of
good drinking time, an inconvenience to be overcome in the
quest for oblivion. Often this 'meal' will be timetabled for later
in the evening, when your face is quite possibly on the wrong
side of your head and it will inevitably consist of random deep-
fried objects carpet-bombed in curry.

It's boom and bust. We fast. We binge. We have the horrors.
We repent. We do it all over again. We will often forgo drinking
until we've built up so much twitching nervous energy, the only
release is to explode in the front door of a pub in a flurry of

twenty-euro notes and broken teeth before knocking back ten shot glasses of something nuclear green and vomiting into the nearest available handbag.

And that'll just be a Tuesday.

We really have a problem.

In Ireland, there are an almost comical number of words to describe inebriation: ossified, plastered, stocious, langers, locked, polluted, half-cut, flootered, congested, paralytic, banjoed, slaughtered, twisted, rat-arsed, legless, gargled, gee-eyed . . . And that's just a list of the ones that have been entered into the Dáil record.

Compare our attitudes to problem drinking here to those in America, for instance.

US Drinkers	Irish Drinkers
Teetotaller	She doesn't drink?!!! What's *wrong* with her?
Six-pack of beer a day	Likes her beer
Functional alcoholic	Enjoys the craic
Clinical alcoholic	Wouldn't be a big drinker
Chronic alcoholic	Bit fond of the drink
Final-stage liver cirrhosis	Dry January?

Saint Patrick's Day in Dublin

Young Irish people seem to be taking on the baton with some flair. They have taken an older generation's penchant for sinking pints and generally tearing the hole out of it to new levels and, with the help of a very supportive drinks industry, they have learnt to adapt it to the world of cheap shots, alcopops and other things that you normally wouldn't put into a car.

One of the best ways to see contemporary Ireland in all its glory is on Paddy's Day in Dublin. It all starts out wonderfully – marching bands from across the globe converge on the capital to celebrate their Irish heritage. Families bring kids into town bedecked in their brightest green, white and orange. It's a wonderful carnival atmosphere for the entire family – you can't move for Derek Mooney and Bláthnaid Ní Chofaigh.

I'll be honest; it's hard not to get a bit misty-eyed. Standing there proudly in your own country, in front of the GPO, flags waving and drums beating, thinking back to all those brave men and women, patriots who fought and died for Ireland, where grown men are now free to cartwheel over O'Connell Bridge dressed as Spiderman.

But then the rot sets in. A cloud suddenly looms over the city at around two o'clock. Within ten minutes, the mood changes from twee, harmless D'Arby O'Giddiness to full-on *28 Days Later*.

Drunken, marauding teenagers emerge toothlessly from sidestreets like extras from *Thriller*, projectile-vomiting in the wake of waddling, frightened Americans. Ossified young women lie orange and upturned on the streets, like lobsters struggling out of water. DART carriages full of pensioners are violently shaken and pushed over by mobs. SWAT teams from the alcohol companies emerge from the skies, abseiling down The Spire to drop emergency crates of cheap cider around loitering hoodies, who are probably plotting awful things to do to your grandmother. By 8 p.m., a state of emergency is usually in place, with frightened Tipperary guards hiding away in Paddywagons, on their knees, praying to Jesus, the saints and anyone else who will listen for one last chance, so they might get through this night of generous overtime alive.

Lads, we seriously have a fucking problem.

A Compendium of Irish Sessions

It is important for you to be prepared for the inevitable onslaught, so with that in mind let's look at some of the most common types of Irish drinking session.

Having a Goo on You

This describes the state of nearly everybody in Ireland at around half four on a Friday afternoon. Workers congregate inside the entrance hallways of offices like runners bursting to start the Dublin Marathon. People on landlines draw doodles of pints of Guinness as they pretend to listen to whoever is talking at them. All they really hear on the other end of the phone is 'Pint pint pint pint pint'. By 4 p.m., senior management are already well gone (and half-cut), having organized a convenient Friday-afternoon 'meeting' off-site. By 4.49 p.m., the place empties like there's been a bomb scare. So once you are in the pub, and the goo is temporarily sated, there are a number of further options available to you.

Going for the One

In other countries, 'the one' is shorthand for your soulmate, the love of your life that you're one day destined to meet and spend the rest of eternity with. In Ireland, 'the one' is shorthand for a pint. Unfortunately, nobody in the history of Ireland has ever managed to go for the one. Because the one inevitably turns into . . .

Two or Three

Two or three pints is considered a fairly light session in Ireland. If the two or three has occurred after a promise to go for the one, then it might end at two or three. Maybe. If, however, the original plan was to have two or three then it will inevitably end up at four or five or even ...

A Feed of Pints

A feed of pints is anywhere between seven and seventeen pints, usually Guinness, which as most of you already know isn't really a drink at all, but more of a dessert. A 'feed of pints' is a purposefully vague term because there is never a way to accurately quantify how many pints have indeed been consumed but it's safe to say you've probably used up much of your alcoholic-unit allowance for the rest of that calendar year.

Doing the Dog on It

'Doing the dog on it' is often what happens at a family function, often when a hotel residents' bar is in place. It marks the point where a feed of pints turns into another feed of pints and where normal activities like speaking in a recognizable language or using a toilet in the traditional way go right out the window. You will, yourself, also end up going right out the window. Other examples of doing the dog on it include buying ten pints of cider just before the bar closes, and Brendan Behan.

On the Absolute Tear

If you have ever read any books about Richard Harris or Brendan Behan you will get some idea of what being 'on the tear' means. It is the alcoholic equivalent of The Crusades. All bets are off. There will be alcoholic carnage at clinically dangerous levels. Any person on the tear will go through a series of drunken phases or visual experiences that are not unlike the Stargate sequence from *2001: A Space Odyssey*. Geographical limitations become null and void. A tear could begin in Shannon, before moving on to West Kerry, then Manchester, before finishing up in, say, Abu Dhabi, frozen and clinging for your life to the landing gear of a passenger jet.

The Hangover

Of course, it would be irresponsible for me to natter on so much about drinking and not detail some of the horrific consequences. Because for every joyous session, there can be hell to pay at the other end. Boom and bust.

Consider yourselves warned.

The Evacuation

The evacuation describes that moment, often early in the morning after a short night of sustained coma, when your body says 'Enough!' and begins to evacuate from the inside without any proper consultation with the owner. In an evacuation, the poison will travel the shortest distance possible in order to escape the human; any orifice will do – the mouth, nose, ears, anus, sometimes it will simply escape through the skin like a pent-up volcano oozing carrots, prior to eruption. Evacuations, when they are made, become explosive physiological events and can often occur dramatically on stairwells as hapless victims lurch headlong in search of a toilet, like Usain Bolt in a photo finish.

The Fear

The fear sets in over the course of a day, usually peaking on a Sunday evening, and often once the physical effects of the hangover have long since departed. Victims have described the fear as the psychological equivalent of processing the entire oeuvre of Franz Kafka in under an hour. Those in the throes of it can often experience deep paranoia and an unnerving heightening of the senses. One man suffering from a particularly bad episode thought he could hear the slow contractions of his colon at a deafening volume. Other victims reported horrifying sensory hallucinations, e.g. being able to smell everything that is happening on *Emmerdale*.

Even the smallest task can turn into a traumatic odyssey during the fear. Ordering takeout on the phone can take on all the weighty significance of the Frost–Nixon interviews. If you do manage to make an order without soiling yourself, you will probably be too afraid to go to the door to collect the food. Instead you'll end up cowering and hungry on the couch, rocking back and forth, in an awful eternal purgatory of *Come Dine With Me* repeats.

Russian Winter

The Russian winter can persist from between four days to a fortnight after the initial poisoning event and is most common in people over thirty. During the Russian winter everything will take on a grey and sullen hue, things that once brought joy – e.g. pets, flowers, your children – cease to feel important any more. As the days progress, your conversations about sports and the weather will be peppered with disturbing jump cuts and slow zooms, like you're trapped in some black-and-white art film. The temperature never rises above −6, even at the height of summer. Eventually though, you will emerge from the freezing fog, shaken but never broken, and usually just in time for Friday night.

The Con-over

The most devious hangover of them all. During the con-over, you will wake up bright eyed, bushy tailed and sometimes with a feeling of mild euphoria. The sun will appear even brighter in the sky. The world is as it should be. And you got away with it! A whole night of boozing and no consequences!

Don't feel so smug, though. The con-over is in the post.

The con-over generally kicks in between 12 noon and 3 p.m., often when you have unwittingly committed to doing something 'useful' with the day. Most likely, when the first signs appear (usually a pulsating eyelid) you will be halfway through dismantling the engine of your car or you will have just arrived at a circus with the kids. For the rest of the day, you will have to live in a Beckettian hell of your own creation, your organs slowly failing as you try to reassemble a gearbox, your soul slowly ascending out of your body as you are picked as the lucky volunteer by the knife-throwing clown.

Plastic Pubs

Ah, there's nothing quite like the cosy warmth of the Irish pub: the sparkling turf fire, the cheerful psychologist/barman holding court behind the taps, the mysterious pub dog wandering around between the stools, licking the slowly decomposing feet of the regulars, not to mention the waft of

lemon urinal cakes drifting in from the toilets. It just feels like
... home.

Then there is the ebb and flow of banter from the old-timers
lining the bar, rising and falling like the movements of a
Wagnerian opera (not to mention the occasional fart for per-
cussive emphasis). You will still find them in every small pub in
the country, sitting face-forward and devout, supping away at
creamy pints of stout, waging war against the remaining oper-
ational capillaries lining their purpled cheeks. There is no place
better to hear about the pressing issues of the day, from 'Who
won the 1953 camogie final and what was unusual about it?'
and 'How far do you think you could throw a medium-sized
pig?' to 'I'd love to hear Sonia O'Sullivan yodel.'

Sure where else would you get it?

Well, anywhere in the world, if certain people had their way.
D'Arby McGinty's, Smelly Nelligan's, Póg Mahoney's, Scutter
Murphy's, The Taj Mícheál, the list goes on ... (consider all
these copyrighted by the way). It's an odd place, the Oirish pub.

Littered with fake roadsigns to an assortment of midlands
shitholes you wouldn't dream of visiting at home and imitation
vintage posters declaring 'Guinness is good for you', the Oirish
pub inevitably has some poor fecker called Pádraig behind the
bar who spends every passing minute of his shift battling
through the crippling irony that he came here in the first place
to try to escape Ireland. The cultural bastardization doesn't end
at fake roadsigns, we've all quietly died inside while reading the
cheesy wall plaques displaying 'ancient' Irish sayings like 'A
good hearth these days is hard to find' and 'When life gives you
lemons, blame the British'.

Once you've submitted to the idea of entering an Oirish
pub, it's vital, at once, to sample and give your opinion on the
Guinness. Whether it's in London, Paris or in some

underground ex-pat watering hole in Abu Dhabi, we almost pride ourselves on the fact that the Guinness, which, let us not forget, is made, sold and distributed by a British company, just isn't as good as it is at home. If two lost Irish people met, parched, in the middle of the Sahara, the first question wouldn't be 'Have you got any water?' but 'How's the pint?' With the inevitable answer being 'Shite'.

Craft-beer Revolution

There are a few beacons of light, however, suggesting we may just be rowing back on the quantity and getting into quality. Nowhere is this clearer than in the craft-beer revolution that's sweeping the nation.

There were always wine snobs in Ireland. You'd spot them occasionally in their cravats and their Bentleys pulling up outside off-licences in a haze of blank cheques and French aftershave. Fortunately, many of these people died off during the banking crisis.

But they have been replaced by a new phenomenon – the Craft-beer Dude.

Craft-beer Dudes, who can be male or female, exclusively wear beards and Norwegian woolly jumpers and are usually seen huddled around colourful bottles at barbecues, often pursing their lips, eyes closed, saying stuff like:

'Well, this one's got an interesting aftertaste, there are real hoppy overtones.'

'Yeah nice. What's it called?'

'Stoat's Liver. What do you think?'

'I think I've gone blind in my left eye.'

Wild Bull Breweries
present
Queen Medb's Fancy
Regal craft beer from the bowels of County Galway

Brewed in Oughterard using our own malted barley and spring water from deep within the Glengowla Mines, this delicious, refreshing golden pale ale has a sweet malt body, sweetened further by a unique process whereby the fermented hops are strained for a month through a 1980's leather Liverpool FC schoolbag stuffed with Wham Bars. Further enriched with a soupçon of cryptosporidium pumped directly from the waters of the Corrib, the sweetness is carefully balanced with a tangy explosion of citrus and the added 'kick' from the subtle infusion of authentic Rosmuck bull semen throughout.

Chapter 8

The Meeja

The media in Ireland is concentrated in the Dublin region and behaves in much the same way as one of those small wind-up toy monkeys that repetitively bangs two cymbals together. It makes an awful clatter in the corner until it eventually runs out of batteries and moves on to the next story.

Here is a brief rundown of some of the major players.

The Irish Times

Considered by many to be the paper of record, particularly by the people who work there, nothing conveys a greater sense of gravitas and self-importance than a folded copy of *The Irish Times* neatly tucked up under the armpit. *The Irish Times* is best browsed awkwardly on trains, ideally while tutting audibly at nearby youths as they cycle repeatedly through mobile ringtones.

Alternatively, it can be left to sit unread next to *The New Yorker* and *Ulysses* on any typical Southside Dublin coffee table, before being rolled up to bat away flies from the dripping glass cornices of last night's chocolate fountain. As well as a staff of full-time journalists, *The Irish Times* also boasts a small army of committed letter writers, renowned the island over for their almost supernatural ability to construct awful puns. These contributors are best observed in their natural habitat, the local library, where they can be found scrunched up over legal pads, giggling forcefully to themselves, their black-rimmed glasses barely held together with electrical tape. Invariably, they will have their lunch in a plastic Centra bag and it will mostly consist of egg.

Yours etc., Reginald, Terenure, Dublin 6W.

RTÉ

Based in the darkest heart of Dublin 4, RTÉ is one of the oldest national broadcasters in the world and in 1743 was the first organization on the planet to perform a radio broadcast – a fight between two dogs that ended in a draw. Often unfairly compared to better-funded British broadcasters, it's easy to forget that RTÉ has been punching well above its weight in recent years having picked up many awards for its drama and current affairs, not to mention the Best Boiled Chicken in a Subsidized Canteen Award for three years running at the Cologne Excellence in Television Catering Expo. RTÉ can count among its many recent successes the magazine show *Nationwide* (a pretty vicious satire on hospital television), the genealogy reality show *How Much Craic Did Your People Have During the Famine?* and *The Late Late Show,* a sort of chat show equivalent to *Forrest Gump,* which just seems to keep on running and running and running and running and nobody has the power to stop it any more.

RTÉ is publicly funded by the TV licence, soon to be renamed the Montrose Levy, but uptake is still slow, with recent inspections reporting that up to a hundred thousand people in Ireland still don't own a TV. This is despite the outline through their front curtains of a big, bright and loud TV-shaped object, which is often hanging at a suspiciously comfortable viewing angle.

Denis O'Brien

As well as owning a veritable shedload of radio stations and a sizeable stake in Independent News & Media, this is only a snapshot of part of Denis O'Brien's growing media empire, which is now believed to be 'bigger than Jesus'. On top of all this, Denis O'Brien holds exclusive rights to the words 'BREAKING' and 'EXCLUSIVE' on the island of Ireland, he owns the key of F sharp major in perpetuity, after outbidding Elton John, and he is even rumoured to have purchased the year 2076 in a deal done with ▓▓ ▓▓▓▓▓ at a Barry Manilow concert last August. It's probably very foolhardy to write this, especially in an increasingly litigious media culture, but I've always held a personal belief that Denis O'Brien's ▓▓▓ ▓ ▓▓▓▓ ▓▓▓ ▓▓▓ hero of the left ▓▓▓ ▓ bursting with flavour ▓▓ ▓ ▓▓ ▓ ▓▓▓

not an invasion of privacy ██████ ███████ █████
notwithstanding the extremely generous serving of chicken
and mushroom vols-au-vent later that evening!

Say what you like about Denis O'Brien . . . oh hang on, actually you can't say what you like about Denis O'Brien.

Local Meeja

Local radio and newspapers are truly the lifeblood of the
national media and Ireland's love of talking about itself,
reflecting on itself and obsessing about itself can be seen here in
deep microcosm. Whether it is pictures of tractors and pigs at a
local agricultural show, the parish notes detailing All The New
Dead People or major incidents of intrigue in the town (e.g. the
disappearance of a swan), local papers treat it all with a solemn
gravity.

These publications can also give world events a profoundly
local twist.

Big Bang in Ballyracket

Excited locals gathered in the town square of Ballyracket last evening to celebrate a momentous launch. Led by local Fianna Fáil councillor and amateur astronomer, Ballyracket-born Tommy 'Worf' Dooley, hundreds gathered for the unveiling of the Big Bang Memorial Statue.

'Using cutting-edge data from the NASA website, the Ballyracket Singularity Committee is delighted to announce that the Big Bang itself has been traced to this very spot in our own little town of Ballyracket, Ireland,' announced Worf Dooley to perplexed applause and at least three

---

crying children. 'This is a historic moment for Ballyracket, for Ireland and for earth, not only placing Ballyracket on the map internationally, but allowing us to claim our rightful place at the very centre of the universe in the run-up to the local elections.'

The statue itself, an apparently limestone rendering of a singularity, completely invisible to the naked eye, sits inside a square area marked off by luminous yellow bollards and a concrete platform designed to replicate the bridge on the USS *Enterprise*. It is thought the council, headed by Worf Dooley himself, have allocated up to five hundred thousand euros of public funds for the construction of this (invisible) memorial.

When asked to confirm how the singularity was traced to Ballyracket, Worf was a little vague, admitting that everywhere in the universe probably sprang from the same point, so the centre of the universe 'wasn't exactly unique to Ballyracket'. However, he followed up by making the point, 'But sure we got there first and isn't that the main thing? Up the Racket!'

Locals were transfixed by the occasion.

Homekeeper Maureen Dwyer enthused: 'It's a wonderful day for all the people of Ballyracket, to find out that, as I suspected, we have been at the centre of the universe all this time. I'm hoping it will create some jobs and maybe my daughter Eileen will move back from the Australian outback where she tends pigs, now things are picking up.'

GAA Public Relations Officer Chesty Maguire added: 'It's good for the parish, good for the club and hopefully we can attract new players. The minor hurlers failed to field last year due to the recession and that's no way for any club to be, especially a proud club like Ballyracket in a little town where the birth of time and space itself took place.'

Proprietor of the local chip shop Toto Macari joked: 'I'm not one bit surprised. If you spent a few weeks here in January, you'd know all about staring into the middle of a fucking black hole.'

NASA has yet to comment.

Online Journalism

As well as traditional media, there is an emerging spate of online media outlets, many of whom operate under the new 'magic beans' business model. Under this system, the 'newspaper' receives one magic bean, or thirty-seven bitcoins, every time some eejit clicks on the awful newsbait and/or listicle they've got some impoverished 'journalist' to generate on the basis that it will look good on their CV. These headlines generally consist of horrific collections of words like 'Kim Kardashian Took Her Puppy to a Gynaecologist – And You'll Never Believe What Happens Next . . .' and 'Ten Super-Cute Meerkats Too Cute to Get Mashed Up in a Combine Harvester'.

Match the Event to the Headline Puzzle

Real Event	Clickbait
Sinking of the *Titanic*	Two Hijacked Planes Full of Suicide Bombers Meet Twin Towers that Became a Symbol of International Capitalism. What Happened Next = EPIC
The Moon Landings	Top 10 Things You Totally Shouldn't Do if You Don't Want to End Up in Hell for Eternity
JFK Assassination	Click Here Now if You Want To Know How To Avoid Freezing to Death in the Middle of the Atlantic Ocean.
God Hands Moses the Commandments on Mount Sinai	What Do an Angry Man in a Book Depository, a Shooter on the Grassy Knoll and a President in an Open-top Car Have in Common? The Answer Will Make Your Head Explode
9/11 Attacks	This Secret TV Studio Footage Will Make You Think You're Walking on the Moon!

Chapter 9

Getting Around

After the Ice Age, when Ireland was mostly covered in ice (see Chapter 4), there followed the Wood Age, a long period when the entire island basically consisted of trees. Geological data suggests that it was an 'absolute pain in the hole' to get from A to B. Branches and trunks and roots would block your every move. Red squirrels would emerge suddenly from behind gorse bushes brandishing muskets. Then, just when you thought it was safe, a wild Irish stag would gallop out from a leafy clearing and kick you square in the face.

It was a harsh, inhospitable and absolutely stupid place.

To make matters worse, there were all the rivers, flowing in vicious torrents in an effort to move the rain out to the sea. These were almost impossible to pass without getting saturated or eaten alive by leeches, eels and weasels. The whole of Ireland was like one of those Hell and Back courses people in offices do nowadays to avoid dying at their desk from advanced muscle atrophy.

Something had to give.

So we cut down all the trees.

Suddenly, a whole new world was opened up. The people of Tipperary could see the people of Limerick and they gave them a wave. The people of Cork and Kerry eyed each other up suspiciously and started firing stones. The people in Meath could look out across all those sprawling counties and see all the new people available to them, to puck with their fists and kick in the shins on the GAA pitch.

It was clear. The people of Ireland wanted to be connected. So a transport infrastructure had to follow – firstly footpaths and dirt roads, eventually canals, rail lines and airports, until such time as we had built up the sophisticated transport network of modern Ireland, which is truly a wonder to behold (as long as you're not living west of the Shannon).

De Roads

Up until relatively recently, Irish politicians spent most of their working lives dealing with complaints, upgrades, resurfacing issues and other general administration relating to the absolute state of the Irish road system. They'd be up all night polishing cat's eyes with buckets of their own spittle and hand-mixing tar coughed up from their own lungs in a valiant effort to fill potholes close to the homes of important constituents. But even they, in their mad quest for votes, couldn't stop the rot.

It got so bad that an official IMF report on Ireland from 1997 found that, on a development scale, the condition of our roads was somewhere between *Mad Max* and the Democratic Republic of Congo.

While most of Central Europe was intersected by great autobahns – giant industrial aortas efficiently pumping the industrial core with lorries full of asparagus, schnitzel and weird German horse porn – up to 58 per cent of the average Irish adult's life was spent angrily queuing behind tractors spewing slurry all over their windscreen.

It was a trying time.

A drive cross-country was often so arduous, and the

challenges so extreme, every dashboard in every car was fes-
tooned with enough religious artefacts to rival Knock, subtly
implying you would probably never ever return. Rosary beads
were drooped over rear-view mirrors. Creepy statues of Saint
Christopher, half-buried in used sick bags, stood glaring at you
for hours, as your dodgy wipers clacked back and forth, like a
metronome counting out the disappearing moments of your
terribly disappointing life. Bottles of holy water would splish-
splash around in glove compartments, patiently awaiting their
deployment during some inevitable last-rites ritual on the side
of the road. Not only did you have to pack blankets, food sup-
plies and water; frankly, it was advisable to leave a will before
you left.

There were good reasons for all this. Firstly, every other
driver on the road, including you, was most likely drunk, especially the guards. There were also the awful surfaces to contend
with, featuring potholes the size of moon craters, and impos-
sible-to-follow signage in various indecipherable dialects of Old
Irish. Grass savannahs grew out of the middle of the tarmac as
if nature itself was embarrassed by the incompetent efforts of
the county council. You had to approach each stage of the
journey like you were the protagonist in some Homeric Odyssey
– the scourge of bottlenecks in places like Abbeyleix and
Durrow and Horse and Jockey that went on longer than the
average menopause and the complete lack of toilets or services
of any sort, leading to regular sightings of lonely motorists on
the roadside literally pissing into the wind, a horrified, blue-
faced child clinging to their backs like a succubus.

So when our own versions of autobahns finally arrived with
their gorgeous, illustrative names – like M8 and M50 and M3
– it was understandable that many people thought the country
was sorted for ever.

But there were teething issues . . .

One couple famously spent over three weeks queuing at the M50 toll booth during the summer of 2002, eventually having to be airlifted from their car, which was filled with half-consumed plastic bottles of their own recycled urine. There is still the outstanding problem of the northwest, a sort of transport Twilight Zone, which is about as easy to reach as the moons of Jupiter (with similar weather conditions). But it is now, finally, possible to get around Ireland fairly easily on the road – welcome news for families and small-business owners, and all the people who like to rob them.

What's the Point?

The penalty-points system has been a success, bringing Irish road behaviour somewhere into line with the rest of civilization, or at least North Africa. This can be hard to accept, especially as you are being cut off on a roundabout by some clown talking on two mobile phones and trying to balance a family-sized bucket of popcorn between their thighs. But the stats, and Gay Byrne, don't lie. So here, by way of a massive diversion and aside – let's call it a bypass – I'd like to propose that this same system be introduced to the rest of social life.

#PenaltyPointsForPricks

Punishment for Unforgiveable Day-to-day Behaviour

People who smoke into your face in bus shelters – 4 pts
Punishment: Go to end of hospital waiting lists.

People who stop abruptly at the top of escalators – 2 pts
Punishment: A hundred flights of stairs.

People who say 'Just heard some great news!' on
Facebook and then don't tell you what it is – 7 pts
Punishment: Cut off their Internet.

People who reveal that a film/book has a 'twist at the
end' – 10 pts
Punishment: Watch *Fast & Furious 18* three times.

People who order a salad and then eat your chips –
12 pts
Punishment: Annulment of marriage.

Fuckers who piss all over toilet seats on trains – 21 pts
Punishment: Have to wear a nappy outside their pants
in public for a week.

People who sit beside you on the bus when there are
many other free seats – 7 pts
Punishment: Three Hail Marys and three Our Fathers.

Hugging the standing rail on a train so nobody else can
use it – 9 pts
Punishment: Have to hug everyone they meet for a
month.

People who walk into you on the street while texting –
13 pts
Punishment: Cut off their phone plans/fingers.

122

Rail

During the late 1800s, the Brits had continued their steady campaign of oppression by installing a national railway network spanning the whole country, connecting aristocrats and ascendancy landlords as far away as West Cork and Westport to the botanical gardens and zoos and afternoon-tea parties and other stuff they were wont to do while the rest of us were busy, I dunno, rooting around in the ditches or shitting into our own hands. The Brits even had the temerity to build a modern tram system in Dublin, which connected the whole of the city in ways modern Dubliners could barely dream of. Unfortunately, immediately after independence, we ripped all this up and ate it. After we were done eating, we took one look at the similarly oppressive canal system and began to fill it up with shopping trolleys.

The modern Irish rail system features various InterCity routes like the Cork–Dublin train, which now takes less than two and a half hours, and the popular Sligo line, which takes less than two and a half days if you 'know the right people'. These trips are often broken up by a bit of light relief – the indecipherable train intercom system, one of the many wonders of Ireland. These announcements boom out of the speakers at regular intervals and at ear-shattering volumes and, depending on the driver, either sound like Big Tom with a pillow over his head or a donkey swallowing its own torso. It will sound something like this.

DIIIIIIIIIING DOOOOOOOOOONG (*Everybody jumps in their seat. Feedback, sound of a microphone being rubbed in someone's crotch*):
   'La'ies and gentlewe'll shorly beerivin' at suckymuurphy

junction, cudge all passengers aloiring at the next stop please discobadgereffluentflapjacks, I repeat, we'll shorly beerivin' at tangobravohoopmutiny, cudge all passengers please p-p-p-pickup-a-penguin now please! THANKEN YOU!'

Tip: You can now handily pre-book your tickets online and include any name you wish on the LED display above your seat. For maximum privacy, I suggest 'Fred West'.

Walking

There's nothing like a good walk. Stretching the legs, blowing out the cobwebs – walking gives you access to the vast splendour and bounty of the great outdoors and it has the added benefit of keeping your mind and body fit, provided you don't get shot in the back by a farmer. Additionally, using your legs is still, at the time of writing anyway, absolutely free and not taxable by the government.

So it remains a fantastic way to see the country.

Walking, or ambulation, can be performed in a variety of ways but in its most basic form it involves vaulting over a stiff limb to propel you forwards in space and time towards, for example, the dole office.

Everyone in Ireland has his or her own unique walk, a personal brand if you will. However, there are a number of broad categories of walk to watch out for on the journey ahead.

The Amble

Popular particularly among District Court judges and nuns, to amble is to walk along slowly with the hands held firmly behind you on the lower back and the snout held aloft, usually at an angle of around 37.4 degrees to the wind. To amble is to sort of slowly think yourself through space and time and it is a walk that commands much respect in the community. It is also the only walk available to GAA umpires for some reason. Unfortunately, in cities, amblers will almost certainly be pulled into a side alley and violently mugged.

The Stomp

The stomp, on the contrary, is a much more agitated, foostering method of walking, involving the hands, legs and other appendages jerking forwards in angular, probing movements towards a destination, e.g. putting a parking ticket on a car. The stomp can often be observed in use by stricter, more by-the-book members of society, such as librarians, ticket inspectors and members of Fine Gael.

WARNING: A man or woman stomping towards you is almost certainly going to want to reprimand you or lecture you on some basic form of civic manners, e.g. 'You should NEVER litter!' 'Seats are not for feet!' 'We'll have no doggers here!'

The Powerwalk

Powerwalkers are generally middle-aged women in luminous-yellow hi-vis jackets and they can be found pounding the roads of rural Ireland, usually moving through the countryside during the hours of dusk, like glow-worms levitating in the twilight. The powerwalk is always accompanied by an air of scandal and general conspiracy, communicated loud and breathlessly over the friendly honks of passing jeeps. These animated conversations will inevitably include such phrases as 'Would you believe he *still* hasn't put up that gate for me?' and 'So anyway, I ordered that three-kilo shipment of chicken goujons on the Internet' and 'Do – Not – Talk – to me about that poisonous cunt at Weight Watchers'.

The Drunkard's Falter

The falter will be on public display every Saturday night in small towns across Ireland and is the perambulation of choice for the badly polluted. In many ways, the falter resembles the action of a leaf being carried in the wind, with the victim often lurching back and forth through space at the mercy of forces beyond their control. Almost miraculously, however, the falterer will also be managing to eat a bag of curry chips and sip from a can of Fanta with a straw, with all the grace of a knife juggler on a unicycle.

Cycling

One of the boons of cycling is that, thanks to recent events in the world of international sport, you now have carte blanche to take as many drugs as you want before getting on a bike. The best places to pick up these drugs are in whatever head shops remain around the country. Some common favourites include: Whang!, an upper that gives you the buzz a South Korean programmer feels after hacking into a major world bank; MoonSoup, taken as a herbal tea and which makes your wrists shrink to the size of pipe cleaners; WHOAMYEYEBALLS!, a unique blend of rat poison mixed with drain-cleaning solution, which makes your eyes roll around in your sockets like snooker balls; and, of course, *The Mind Adventures of Solomon Carruthers*, a book which, when licked, transports you back to the year 1587 where you get to act as first admiral of the Portuguese navy for a fortnight.

Obviously, you can also just cycle clean, but it's your loss. There are few sights in Ireland more moving than the Conor Pass as you freewheel down it on methamphetamine.

Somehow, despite all this, the typical cyclist is a smug, self-righteous Stalinist who tends towards the conclusion that they own the road. They also think they own the footpaths. And supermarket aisles. And one-way streets even when they are cycling the wrong way down them.

So, you should never approach cyclists in your car when they're moving ten abreast up a narrow mountainous road or collectively breaking another red traffic light in the city. They'll circle and swarm your vehicle and eventually savage you like a shoal of hungry piranha.

Remember, they own the road.

Airports

There was a time in Ireland when air travel was considered out of reach for the working person (apart from those who won a holiday on *Where in the World?* presented by Theresa Lowe). Flying was the preserve of the super-rich elite, people like Roger Moore, Grace Jones and Pádraig Flynn. Everyone else had two options: either take the ferry or stay in bed and die.

At that time, Aer Lingus air hostesses were so highly thought of, and the allure of their feline-green mystique so appealing, they would regularly be allowed to sit on Charlie Haughey's knee in first class.

Nowadays, of course, these people are at best referred to as 'cabin staff' and at worst 'trolley dollies' and they spend much of their time herding English stag parties down off the wings and back on to the plane before take-off.

Modern aviation is cheap as chips and can be stressful for the average traveller. Before the plane even takes off, it is prudent to do some customary profiling of your fellow passengers. Sure, that morbidly obese priest looks kindly but for all you know that's a bomb stitched into his belly. You know that the mildly tanned builder from Wexford probably isn't a mujahedeen, but can you be sure? How can you be certain that toddler doesn't have a rattle filled with anthrax?

We can't even trust the pilots any more. Once you're in the cabin, you'll be trying to tell if he's going to sabotage the plane mid-flight just by the way he might be holding his Styrofoam cup.

But, as every Irish person knows, being able to get off the island quickly and cheaply is a vital option to have available to you. So we put up with it. But now with Aer Lingus out of public ownership and Ryanair undergoing a radical change of image, there may be room in the market for a new player.

So I give you new entrants, the Cavan-based low-fares airline, Avarice Air.

AVARICE AIR
AGM Minutes
09/03/2015

In attendance
CEO Moore Power
CFO Podge Sullivan
Head of Creative Kimberly Wingspan
Secretary Agnes Coughlan

I Call to order
Moore Power calls to order the annual general meeting of Avarice Air at 10.35 a.m. on 09/03/2015 at Avarice Air HQ, Cootehill Business Park, Co. Cavan.

II Approval of minutes from last meeting
Agnes Coughlan reads the minutes from the last meeting. The minutes are quickly approved as read by MP who also stresses he has a golf classic at 1 p.m.

III Open issues

a) On recent Air Accident Investigation Unit report 426EF-NinerNinerDelta

Podge Sullivan makes suggestion to discuss the recent complaint against AA pilots for turning off engines and gliding planes into Dublin to save money on fuel, in contravention of current regulations. MP makes wanking gesture. (*Laughter*) MP says that the stupid f***ers should get their nose out of our business, the amount of fuel we f***ing save during those descents is the only thing keeping our head above water FFS. PS mentions that further breaches will involve significant fines. MP repeats sentence back at him sarcastically in a child's voice. (*Laughter*) PS says he will take issue up with pilots' unions. MP advises him to take up issue 'with your mother'.

b) Pilots' union issues

PS notes useful segue to issue of pilots' unions. MP makes another wanking gesture. (*Laughter*) PS notes unions have again brought up issue of breach in European working directives vis-à-vis AA pilots. MP says 'When did we ever recognize f***ing unions? It's pricks like those kept this country in the shithouse for decades.' MP then addresses head of creative and asks if 'anything can be done on the pilot problem'. Kimberly Wingspan says she has been looking at issue of getting rid of pilots completely. PS interrupts, saying no way regulations will allow for cabin crew to fly planes. KW interrupts to say she has market research to show that, in the future, passengers could be convinced to fly planes themselves in exchange for e.g. a lifetime of reduced fares, free alcohol in bags. MP suggests we should blue-sky this more at next meeting. He winks at KW, says he 'likes the cut of her jib' etc.

IV New business

a) Cost-cutting

MP brings up issues of further cost-cutting. 'Is there anything further we can cut, lads?' PS says we may be looking at diminishing returns and bad press if we proceed with plan to charge €500 for late check-in. Also says Health & Safety has pooh-poohed MP's 'catacomb' idea to stack passengers in columns to make more room in the cabin. MP makes wanking gesture. (*Laughter*) MP calls for immediate brainstorming session. More doughnuts wheeled in. PS comes up with notion that ALL future European flights could be landed at one hub, e.g. Amsterdam, and passengers could make their way from there to individual destinations. MP likes this, but says it's a bit pedestrian. MP suddenly puts question to room:

130

'Do we even need f***ing planes anyway?' (*Silence*) MP wonders if people even need to travel. 'Who needs a pointless stressful holiday, surrounded by monstrous kids, when you could be relaxing at home? Couldn't all those half-arsed business meetings be discussed on Skype?' MP wonders if there is a 'no-fares' model. PS looks at MP like he's got more than one head. KW surmises whether people might pay a small charge NOT to go on holidays. MP loves this and calls her 'a f***ing genius'. Asks her to compile a report at next meeting re. no-fares concept.

V Any other business

a) Doughnuts

MP leaves abruptly for golf classic. PS collects money from all present to cover cost of doughnuts etc.

VI Adjournment
PS adjourns the meeting at 12.55 p.m.

Minutes submitted by: Agnes Coughlan

Chapter 10

Politics and Economy

In a recent survey of the Irish electorate entitled 'Voter Apathy – A Long-worded Study on Same Conducted for an Extortionate Fee by Some Market-research Company Funded by You, the Taxpayer', a young man from Mayo, who shall remain nameless, was asked to sum up his current attitude towards Irish politics. Bernard stopped to think for a moment, then let out a sigh so long and drawn out, in a tone so extraordinarily weary and containing feelings of such deep-seated, crushing cynicism, that the small area of space and time around him began to spool inwards as he drew the breath back in, creating a temporary black hole around his face and neck that began to suck in everything for miles around: the market researcher and her clipboard; a Eurospar containing three pensioners and an Indian gentleman; about fourteen Toyota Corollas with dogs inside; and finally, Bernard himself, whose lower regions ended up all mangled up inside his own face.

You can't blame him really. The people are angry. The main message that politicians seem to be receiving on the doorsteps these days is 'Get the fuck off my doorstep'. It's a frightening time for democracy and those who were guaranteed a political career because of who their father was and what he did with the roads.

Even though they say that all political careers end in failure, in recent years, many Irish political careers have tended to start and middle in failure too. It's fair to say that the consistent banjaxing of the country at the hands of a political class, many of whom have shit where their brains should be, has led people to become a tiny bit disillusioned with the process. Many even resort to making horrifying statements like 'They should let Michael O'Leary run the country'.

How on earth did we get here?

Stroke Politics

In a stroke, poor bloodflow to the brain causes one side of the body politic to become completely paralysed as the victim's moral compass splits violently in two, one side retaining the truth concerning any situation, while the other side completely ignores that in pursuit of a 'higher good', e.g. having works done on one of your holiday homes in return for a speedy passport application. Strokes have been the lifeblood of Irish politics for many years and the tradition continues ever still.

The Nod and the Wink

'Say nothing, I'll sort you out, leave it with me.'

A close relation of the stroke, the nod and the wink describes a synchronized movement of the neck and eyelid which dynamically communicates an assurance to the constituent that whatever is being done to address their current need will most definitely be done but should never be discussed in public, as what is about to be done is also likely to be completely illegal.

Auction Politics

Auction politics explains the mad-eyed desperate leer of all politicians in the run-up to any general election. It particularly applies to incumbent governments who have to make one last desperate attempt to win voters over in order to mask the growing list of their accumulated failures. No matter how it might affect the long-term well-being of the nation, parties will fall over themselves making promises they can never keep, usually involving generous tax cuts, partnership deals, free cheese, handjobs, etc. etc. etc.

Lies

Over the years, the Irish electorate has been deceived, lied to and bullshitted in myriad creative ways. Indeed, lying has become a vital part of the political skillset and there is a raft of options available.

Little White Lies
These tiny, minuscule lies matter very little in the grand scheme of things and are often told completely unnecessarily. An example from everyday life is 'I'll get you a pint the next time'. They are often described as harmless but little white lies do serve to contribute to a general aura of dishonesty/bullshit in a given society (Ireland).
Telltale signs: A distinct smirk/sneer.
Example: Almost anything uttered during a tribunal of inquiry.

Tall Stories

These are fairly ridiculous lies, too close to the truth to be dismissed outright, but which any reasonable person could identify as distinctly fishy from the outset.

Telltale signs: Wide eyes, gesticulating in the air.

Example: 'The dog ate my homework.'

Casting Aspersions

These are very tactical falsehoods utilized to casually put someone else 'in it'.

Telltale signs: Pointing and shrugging, quivering eyebrows.

Example: 'Sure, didn't we inherit this whole mess from the previous government?!'

Proper Bullshit

This is a very creative category of lie, adored by low-level psychopaths and property developers. During proper bullshit, not only do you suppress the truth, you also create a whole new scenario from the murky depths of your Machiavellian imaginings.

Telltale signs: Comb-over stands erect on head as if it is, itself, aware of the lie.

Example: 'There's no way we could have known that the property market would go belly up. It was utterly unforeseeable. The insinuation that I displayed any irresponsibility in the establishment of a consortium to develop the Olympus Mons area of Mars using the savings of forty Irish dairy farmers is gross libel which I, or my crack team of barristers, will not tolerate. Are you going to Cheltenham this year?'

Selective Memory

Using selective memory, you lead people down the garden path of your own implied virtuousness by volunteering a few morsels of actual fact while ignoring some significant elephants in the room.

Telltale signs: Playing with necktie, sweating around the nipples.

Example: 'On the night of the bank guarantee, I happened across two sick baby blackbirds, lying by the canal. After innocently guaranteeing the debts of foreign speculators with public money, I took the blackbirds home and nursed them back to health. The following Monday, I set them free.'

The Whopper

All and sundry will know a whopper for what it is in an instant – a massive, glaring lie. The person dropping a whopper (the whoppee) is basically performing a sort of performance lie – they may as well have a pointy hat on their head with 'I'm a total liar!' written on it. The whopper contains such dangerously high doses of horse-shit and spoofery that committing whoppers can even become addictive. Indeed, on the basis of some tribunal evidence it's fair to say that once you whopp, you just can't stop.

Telltale signs: Frothing at the mouth, edging away from you as they tell it.

Example: 'I found the money under a hedge.'

Nepotism

A recent DNA buccal swab test of a random group of politicians in Dáil Éireann revealed the genetic pool to have all the diversity of a remote Mississippi swamp. However, the results of this test are contentious given that it was carried out by an unqualified cousin of a junior minister for €25,000 in cash and some free printing.

For many years in Ireland, it wasn't really what you knew, or who you knew, but who you were related to. Many of these families are still there today, like a strain of dormant malaria in some tropical forest, adapting away in the dark edges, becoming ever more virulent by the day, until they are ready to enter the world again, most likely in a brand-new host body wearing a fantastic suit.

But that is all in the past. (Isn't it?) Gone are the days when a politician would march up to you with their underpants protruding and a bit of rasher stuck to their chin to ask you for your vote. Most contemporary politicians are stage-managed within an inch of their lives, from the words they use (going forward, burden-sharing, in the common interest, etc.) to the clothes they wear (eh, suits). They've even stopped giving some of them the bumps after they've won a seat, which was always a bit of a giveaway as to how they might behave in office.

But does it really matter? The truth is that civil servants run Ireland anyway. Yet nobody has really figured out who these people are, what they do or indeed how the hell we are going to afford them in the future.

Public Sector Pay Grade Scale Chart 2015/2016

Assistant Principal (Higher)
€65,000 *Assessment: Solitaire (Windows 95 vers.)*

Principal
€75,647 *Assessment: Snap, Pontoon*

Principal (Higher)
€81,080 *Assessment: Pac-Man (completed)*

Assistant Secretary
€119,572 *Assessment: Foundation Level Irish*

Deputy Secretary
€156,380 *Assessment: Guess Who?*

Secretary General III
€167,300, *Assessment: Minesweeper (>2147483648 pts)*

Secretary General II
€176,350 *Assessment: Candy Crush (Easter Bunny Hills)*

Secretary General I
€185,350 *Assessment: Angry Birds (King Pig level)*

Perhaps though, we can look to the various parties for an answer. What unique visions of Ireland do they offer? What hope can they give?

The Garden of Ireland

Political speeches are often full of gardening metaphors. Sowing seeds of change, creating sustainable growth, replenishing the soil, cutting back in order to grow again, green shoots, etc. etc. etc. With this in mind, let's have a look at the various political choices available to us today by thinking of Ireland as a small garden, the political parties as gardeners and how you might explain the entire political landscape to a small child on a swing eating a lollipop.

Fianna Fáil

For many years Fianna Fáil trusted in the natural flora of the Irish landscape, letting The Garden grow wild and free and letting the Children of Ireland roam around it. They planted many native species of tree, hedge and flower and over time it became a fabulous, colourful habitat for bees and frogs, bedecked with multicoloured wildflowers and it all pretty much took care of itself. Fianna Fáil watched on from a tent with a bottle of Powers and a packet of Rothmans, often playing poker. Unfortunately, after many years of neglect and no forward planning to speak of, natural growth and prosperity turned The Garden into an untameable wilderness. So much so that one morning, a heavily congested Fianna Fáil woke up to discover that The Bear had made its home at the bottom of The Garden and had mauled the Children of Ireland during the night.

The Progressive Democrats

While Fianna Fáil was leaving The Garden to grow wild, the PDs created a small area consisting mostly of tarmac and artificial grass to the side of the fence. Here, they set up a small Garden Centre selling off the produce of The Garden from a stall by the roadside. While The Garden continued to grow unruly and just before The Bear moved in, the PDs sold their stake in the Garden Centre to a Sino-Russian consortium at a massive profit and moved to Portugal where they now live on a golf resort.

Fine Gael

After Fianna Fáil abandoned The Garden and went off to town to collect its pension and drown its sorrows in the pub, Fine Gael took it over, not for the first time, when it was very badly overgrown and covered in the blood of the recently savaged Children of Ireland. Fine Gael started off by shooting The Bear in the face and forcing the rest of the Children of Ireland to move to another garden. It then embarked on a process of hacking, cutting, slashing and burning which it set about doing with a fervour bordering on sexual. It uprooted all the native Irish trees and sold them off to Donald Trump who now uses them as as wig stands.

Labour

Labour was hired by Fine Gael to do a lot of heavy lifting after the incident involving The Bear. They were very effective labourers for Fine Gael. They helped clear out much of the hard-to-move middle ground in The Garden and spent much of their time in the front drive trying to convince passers-by that the smoke rising from behind the house wasn't as bad as it looked and that they were doing what they could to minimize the carnage. Eventually, sick of their crowing, everyone started pelting Labour, throwing stones from their cars.

Sinn Féin

Sinn Féin patrols a small area of The Garden that is actually behind the wall to an adjoining property. This is a disputed area of The Garden and it is full of many suspicious-looking mounds under which things are quite possibly buried. Sinn Féin have planted lots of pretty flowers to cover over the mounds, but people find it hard to tear their gaze away from them. Unperturbed, Gerry Adams continues to tweet diverting pictures of his cute little dog in The Garden. Sinn Féin might one day be considered contenders to run The Garden, but then again, mounds.

Independents

The Independents are mainly concerned with very small and specific issues relating to The Garden. In general they will make a big racket about tiny subjects, e.g. 'This wall should be over there!' 'I'll not have a windmill in my backyard!' 'We have every right to cut that turf!' The Independents are increasingly popular, mainly because the establishment gardeners have been killing the plants by over-pruning. But would they manage to run The Garden for more than five minutes without impaling each other with pikes?

Greens

The Greens are atypical among political parties in that they might actually have the knowledge to successfully run The Garden. No doubt they have the tools and enthusiasm to make it a successful, sustainable place for us all to enjoy. Unfortunately, the Greens *did* get a chance to run The Garden and although they managed to grow a few spectacular sunflowers, they never noticed The Huge Bear sitting there, shitting in the woods as they were working.

United Left Alliance

The ULA believes The Garden should be operated as a communal space where everybody works together to create a sustainable future for all, where all wealth is shared equally and where little fluffy bunnies hop around in Che Guevara T-shirts smoking pipes. Unfortunately, the ULA have never done a day of actual gardening in their entire lives.

Filling the Political Vacuum

With establishment parties in free fall there's never been a better time for new voices to pitch in and earn the right to run The Garden. These new alternatives are popping up every other day.

Renua: Not to be confused with the PDs, Renua wishes to reopen the Garden Centre at the side of the garden with Eddie Hobbs behind the counter.

Regressive Diplomats: An exciting new proposition, the RDs are a series of retired ambassadors who sit around in nappies, wailing and flinging poo at one another. They could be a serious threat to Fianna Fáil's core vote.

Fine Fáil: Combining Fine Gael's right-of-centre conservatism with Fianna Fáil's one-of-a-kind brand of right-wing socialism, this is basically civil-war politics gone mental.

Fianna Gael: Like Fianna Fáil only with more farmers. They will also bring specific Fine Gael tendencies to the table, e.g. licking their thumbs before turning the pages of a book.

The People Before the People Before Profit: The Garden's first ever far-right party, the PBPBP is mostly inspired by UKIP and hope to erect huge fences and CCTV around The Garden, to keep Ireland Irish.

I Can't Believe it's Not the Real IRA: More mounds, I suppose.

It's the Economy, Ya Big Eejit!

The Irish economy has been the subject of intense international monitoring over recent years, in much the same way any serious car accident will be curiously rubbernecked by all passing motorists. We are the classic rags-to-riches-to-rags-to-riches-to-rags-to-rags-to-riches story. We've had a whole plethora of Bond villain-types in, anxious to stop us making a pig's hoop of it all again. Or that's what they say they're up to, anyway. These mysterious organizations include the IMF, the ECB, the KLF, a bunch of increasingly moody ratings agencies, not to mention a whole host of large accountancy firms including KPMG and Crosby, Stills, Nash, Ernst & Young.

The Celtic Tiger saw a huge shift in the way we do business, from a period when we mostly spat into our hands, wiped snot off our noses, then shook on things to a new era whereby we play the role of a sort of low-tax gimp nation for a range of shiny global corporations, whose attitude to us is probably best summed up by the phrase 'squeal like a piggy'.

There are many arguments as to what sort of economy we actually have in Ireland. Some (people on the left) say that we live under an unfair right-wing, pro-business regime. Others (people on the right) say we are in fact highly redistributive and have a far more equal system than many people would admit.

They're all wrong.

Irish economics is, in truth, a bit more of a 'wrong-wing' system. It is so far to the right of centre that it actually reaches a point where it travels all the way around and meets up with the far left again. Basically, it's off the scale. In Ireland, we are experimenting with a brand-new idea called trickle-up economics, the brainchild of the celebrity economist Milton Keynes, the bastard child of right-wing monetarist Milton Friedman and the more interventionist J. M. Keynes, which combines all the most egregious elements of capitalism – the enrichment of a small class of the super-wealthy who keep getting richer – with the most childishly utopian elements of communism: having a million theories about the distribution of cake without having any recipe for it. Under this new system it is hoped that, over time, the small amount of wealth and savings built up by the middle classes under austerity will eventually trickle up to the filthy-rich yacht-wanker class who have been so badly hurt by the global financial crisis. Once this money filters up, it is then *hoped* – because remember economics isn't a science – that the cheering effect this will have on the sort of well-oiled psychopaths who regularly go to Cirque du Soleil concerts with escorts could cause the money to simply cascade down through the system again, creating a new boom in world finance and ushering in a golden era of growth, spending and wealth

146

creation, which will eventually filter back down to the working classes in the form of jobs – if they're not all dead.

Anyway, I suppose we'll see how that goes.

**Every time I hear the words 'Quantitative Easing'
I sing it to the tune of Marvin Gaye's 'Sexual Healing'.
It's getting me through the recession.**

Chapter 11

The Arts

It is not very well understood, but for some reason many Irish people display an innately artistic sensibility. Whether in music, theatre, film, literature or the wildly innovative creativity on display in our corporate-accountancy sector, we tend to punch well above our weight. I will outline a few of the most popular forms here, starting with the most famous of all . . .

Dancing

Anyone who's ever been to Dublin on a visit knows the Irish love a dance. And we are famous throughout the world for our unique traditional dancing, which comes in a range of unforgettable styles.

The Céilí

With their highly aggressive, often militaristic titles, like 'The Siege of Ennis', 'The Walls of Limerick' and 'Thirteen Massive Heart Attacks Just Waiting To Happen', céilí dances are a form of social dancing consisting of various mysterious, impossible-to-remember steps requiring little or no skill, often performed opposite heavily sweating relatives at family functions. (Although, it's arguable whether 'social dancing' is an appropriate term for getting randomly pole-axed by your auntie Assumpta.)

Thankfully, Irish people of all ages are well able to handle the rabid intensity of céilís. This is primarily down to a rare marker in our DNA called the TX123-123-123-Heel-Push-Forwards-123-123 chromosome. However, visitors should tread very carefully (literally). The sudden movements and waves of energy at a céilí dance can be overwhelming and the craic can sometimes reach dangerous levels (below ninety is generally considered safe). In one particularly famous example, a wedding reception in a Cavan hotel rose to such a glorious crescendo that the building had actually edged about fifteen miles down the road by the time everyone got up the following morning. Ten cars and a family of herons were completely destroyed in the process.

Sean-nós

Sean-nós dancing, on the other hand, is a relaxed sort of improvised dancing that doesn't really follow any rules at all. It's the dancing equivalent of going for a quick pint in the afternoon. Sean-nós dancers have been known to keep both feet completely off the ground for up to fifteen minutes, a form of jaunty levitation. They achieve this by creating a small parcel of air directly underneath the feet from the swirling convection currents they generate using fluctuating temperatures in each of their toes, a mysterious craft that has been passed down through the generations. They are also renowned meditators. Master dancers become so transcendent, they have been known to reach a state of pure nirvana as they perform. During the 1970s, one Sligo man was found to be still dancing even though doctors estimated he had been clinically dead for at least three days. The slowly accumulating smell of decomposition and hints of rigor mortis were the only signs that eventually alerted members of the studio audience.

Riverdancing

'Riverdancing' first emerged in Ireland well before the natives discovered fire and is believed to have initially evolved as a way to keep people warm during winter cold snaps. Through trial and error, the Irish discovered that dancing violently on the spot until your feet turned bloody could, in fact, act as a very effective natural insulator.

In Irish dancing, the upper body is controlled and rigid, with the arms and back held straight, while the legs tend to flail about like they are actively trying to escape from the torso. It is often accompanied by the loud and raucous sound of clacking, not unlike a particularly violent drive-by shooting. Nobody really knows why it evolved that way. Some believe that the person who invented Irish dancing may have been paralysed from the hips up. Others believe it was a quirky quest by druids seeking to unearth the least sexually desirable form of movement in the entire universe. Most agree though, that, like many Irish innovations, it was often used as a crude defence mechanism against the British. It was hoped that by teaching young boys and girls to hold themselves upright and motionless, followed by a sudden explosion of kicking with the speed and force of about a thousand horses, they could be effective in guerrilla warfare against the marauding forces of empire.

Of course, there is also the possibility that people just fancied an aul' boogie.

Whatever the origins, becoming an Irish dancer is no cakewalk. Many naive tourists return home thinking they can simply take up Irish dancing as a hobby. Be careful. You think training with the Royal Ballet is tough? Think being an active member of ISIS demands commitment? You know *nothing*.

Irish dancers are trained on remote rural boot camps where they are kept in climate-controlled enclosures with underfloor heating that can be raised to searing temperatures to force them to keep their feet off the ground. At night, these trainee dancers sleep in giant leather stirrups, suspended from the rafters. This stops their leg muscles seizing up and also prevents them from escaping. Their days often consist of intensive fourteen-hour classes on technique, endurance and bowel control at the hands of psychopathic dance teachers with names like Ursula and Gobnait. They even import some of these teachers from rural America now – intense taskmasters who pull together a horrifying skillset combining the strict discipline of the US military with the *Full Metal Jacket* intensity of Irish-dancing teaching culture. Students are often beaten round the soles of their feet with hurleys so they develop the calluses necessary to withstand the friction of their feet hitting the floor at a rate of over 180bpm. Indeed, it is thought that the force exerted on the floor by an average Irish dancer over the course of a typical jig is the weight equivalent of an articulated lorry resting on the shins of a baby.

Dancers also need strong hearts. They are often raised on a diet of cocaine and Sunny Delight to develop the coronary muscles necessary to withstand the almost superhuman levels of exertion on their respective systems. Other, more psychological, side effects of this intense training also become inevitable.

Few of us can forget the heart-breaking case of Iarla Thadhg Cáit Ní Chionnara, a fourteen-year-old boy who trained so hard for the Fleadh Cheoil of 1982 he was found to have developed hooves by the morning of the competition.

Shamefully, he was disqualified from the competition that year because of an antiquated law banning livestock from entering. He returned, inconsolable, to his pen that night where he danced himself to death in protest, wearing a pair of heavy Dutch clogs.

Literature

If you've managed to successfully stick with this book until now, you'll be shocked to learn that Ireland is famous the world over for its literary tradition, a tradition I am now going to summarize quickly before *The Simpsons* starts.

Dublin – City of Bukes

Walk around Dublin today and you simply can't get away from the deep tug of literary history. Amble by the Abbey and you can almost feel the ghostly presence of W. B. Yeats. Walk down any side street and it's quite probable that Brendan Behan once stood there, urinating down a gable wall, fag hanging from his upper lip. You might even encounter the benign spirit of Maeve Binchy drifting through the aisles at Avoca.

Many tourists would get the impression that Dublin is a city steeped in books.

It was once, actually.

During the Great Book Floods of 1887, the personal library of the aristocrat Sir Thomas Sigmund Sibelius McCarthy became so very overcrowded it started to spill out of the ornate, stained-glass doorway of his Georgian residence, going on to flood the entire city centre, drowning street urchins in a sea of knowledge and creating a wave of words that eventually reached a height of over six feet. Thousands of Dubliners were forced to stand on the spot for days, surrounded by a smothering quicksand of Russian tomes, books on ornithology and steamy French novellas, until they were eventually pulled away from the growing avalanche of dangerous and potentially mind-expanding knowledge by a crack team of Catholic priests.

But Dublin's literary past is a very real thing. This is, after all, the very city whose day-to-day life was microscopically celebrated in *Ulysses*, a book so mind-bendingly brilliant and daring I really must get around to finishing it one day.

Sadly, official Ireland usually treated many of the great writers – whom we now like to put on stamps and name bridges after – extremely poorly.

Here's the basic template:

- A great artistic talent is conceived in Ireland. This is the putative writer's first introduction to sex.
- Ireland gives the talented young person three of the greatest gifts a writer can receive: a world-class education, Hiberno-English and sexual repression.
- The writer is forced into penury in one way or another, either by being fired from a state job for having written about sex, having their entire work banned because it's about sex or simply for appearing to be maybe thinking about sex.
- The writer escapes to some European or North African capital, where he/she has been so hurt by Ireland they are forced to write and obsess exclusively about Ireland for the rest of their days. They invariably get to have lots of sex during this time.
- The writer gains great notoriety and acclaim on the world stage. More sex follows.
- An Irish politician, who hasn't had sex in a month,

opens a public monument named after the writer without consulting the writer's family, a monument on which many drunken people will probably have outdoor sex.

How to Spot an Irish Novelist

Much has changed. A tough profession to break into, becoming an Irish writer nowadays can be a very creatively rewarding/ tax-efficient career. You are unlikely to be forced into exile and there are a range of genres you can choose between: difficult poetry that absolutely nobody will read, all that Booker Prize-nominated literary fiction that people know they probably should read and that badly written S&M-themed stuff about vampires and whipping and secret societies in the South of France that everyone secretly reads.

But writing can be very taxing, even if it is tax-free. Words have to follow on from other words and these words are often quite reasonably expected to form into some sort of coherent sentence which itself leads on to a paragraph that moves the story along, hopefully maintaining the reader's interest. This may sound easy, but that last sentence took me a whole morning to formulate and it still isn't right. And that was after three bouts of aggressive hoovering, an unnecessary trip to the butcher's and an argument on the Internet with a complete stranger.

Writing is hard.

Literary writers can frequently be seen out and about in Ireland and there are a few telltale signs for spotters. They will most often be observed donning long black overcoats and walking along high ridges above desolate towns, scanning the local geography and slowly populating the streets with fascinating, complex characters drawn from deep within their imaginations.

Literary writers often have deep ridgelines across their faces and foreheads. The pupils of their eyes shine vibrantly and can pierce through their subjects with an unimpeachable wisdom, in much the same way Vulcans and social-welfare assessment officers do. They will often speak slowly and methodically, and the words fall out of their mouth and on to the page, each a little fully formed child made of ink. They almost all, men and women alike, possess a fine head of Irish Writer's Hair™ which has thickly matted together after decades of worry and now sweeps up from their foreheads in cascading grey waves, which rise and fall like fizzing Atlantic swells (tip: Head & Shoulders). On weekend mornings, they often stride into taverns and restaurants in that writerly way, cloaked in mystery and pipe smoke, always lost in observational reverie. They visit local hospitals and the cold kitchens of farmers on field trips, where they sit and observe regular people confronting contemporary themes, e.g. death/emigration/death. They sit back in the shadows, coldly analysing the small spaces in conversations, attaching great significance to quotidian activities, how the everyman or woman might brandish an iron or clench the remote control of a Sky box. It gets a bit awkward, after a while, so you should just ask them to leave.

Music

Music, as a basic concept, was first discovered by a talented Irish caveman called Hup! in or around the Kilfenora area of County Clare. You see, Hup! was struggling to start a fire by banging two large lumps of rock together. But no sparks emerged. However, through repeated rhythmic banging and syncopation over many days, Hup! made a new and startling discovery. He

157

had accidentally stumbled across 9/8 time and the slip jig.

Hup! became caught up in a whirligig of pure joy. He got a fierce buzz from these primal rhythmic pulses. He just couldn't wait to tell the rest of his tribe about this new invention. Sadly, three days later, Hup! froze to death on the side of a cliff, but his wife Yeeeehooooooo! and their three children Gwan!, Rise It! and Fair Play Christy! carried on the tradition and thus started the Kilfenora Céilí Band and the incredible story of Irish music, or diddly-aye, as ignorant fuckers tend to call it.

Rich Tradition

The building blocks of Irish traditional music – jigs, reels, slow airs and beards – developed in Ireland over many centuries, with a strong North African influence. The music that resulted is one of the richest seams of Irish culture: the subtle inflections of sean-nós singing, with songs that can go on for months; the intricate dance music of Sliabh Luachra, which slides and polkas its way around the houses; not to mention all that East Clare fiddling.

The truth is, Irish traditional music has influenced world music like few others. When emigrants were forced to leave these shores throughout our history, they didn't just take their suitcases; they took with them all the music and associated folklore passed down to them by their forefathers, packed away inside their heads. And cholera.

But it was the music that lasted and it went on to influence everything from rock to jazz to American country. You hear its echoes today in Appalachian old-time music and bluegrass, in the London folk-punk of The Pogues, in Morrissey's quiet sense of disappointment and it couldn't be clearer than in the 'toora loora looras' of a thousand drunken Santas.

Embarrassing Tradition

Of course, the nuances of all this are lost somehow when you see a grown man in a leprechaun suit playing an electric fiddle in that great second branch of traditional Irish music – the Eurovision.

The Eurovision is our annual reminder that we really need to keep a line of communication open with the Americans.

It is a competition that is almost doubled over under the creaking weight of its own irony, not to mention the weird, unfathomable politics of those Eastern European voting blocs. It's easy to forget it, but for a long time the Eurovision Song Contest was the only actual reason for Ireland to continue as a democratic project. This peaked in the 1980s when Johnny Logan won the competition twelve times in under a decade and more or less bankrupted the country, financially and spiritually.

This talent for making mildly embarrassing music continued on well into the 1990s. For many years, it was a widely known fact that the slowest male of an Irish household would be sent into the priesthood, being unfit for the world of work. In much the same way, for much of the 1990s, all good-looking young males of questionable intelligence were packed off into boy bands, requiring not a solitary electron of talent. There followed much fame, miming and gazing out longingly into cameras, usually while clutching something invisible around the chest area.

Unfortunately though, it all dried up over time and the live register has since become overladen with a huge glut of gorgeous idiots, who now have far fewer places to showcase their complete and utter lack of talent. Sure, there are all those weekend TV talent shows, with the Nuremberg Rally-type feel to them, but even these now insist on some fundamental tricks of the trade, like being able to hold a note, click your fingers together in time or effectively fellate a member of the judging panel backstage.

Sadly, many of these people can now only sit around shopping centres as unpaid eye candy, vacuously pursing their lips, as they get ready to order yet another smoothie, while time and entropy gnaw away slowly at those hot, protruding cheekbones.

Chapter 12

A Sporting People

A recent questionnaire taken by a randomly polled group of two hundred Irish adults found that, before even answering the first question, 68 per cent of them had shot out the door with a hurley to repeatedly puck a sliotar against a gable wall. Make no mistake about it, we're sports MAD.

Sport can unite the nation like few other things. The temporary opening up of Croke Park to rugby and soccer bridged more cultural divides than a thousand well-intentioned Abbey Theatre plays. Indeed, it is thought the sight of John Hayes crying to 'Amhrán na bhFiann' was *so* very moving, and *so* deeply healing, the actual geography of Ireland changed as a result. Seismologists have measured that the country physically moved five feet closer to Britain and sped-up footage of this tectonic shift clearly shows the island of Ireland making a 'bring it in' gesture across the Irish Sea.

Every year, Irish people the globe over gather together for that wonderful shared experience of the diaspora – the All-Ireland Finals. For the very lucky ones, Marty Morrissey may even give you a shout-out on live television: 'We say hello to Father Dunny O'Driscoll, tuning in from Namibia and shouting on the men from The Banner today. We send greetings also to Sharon from Tubbercurry who's watching today's match on a couch in her Sydney apartment after what was a long and immensely pleasurable one-night stand with an Israeli munitions officer called Beni. Finally, we say hello to Sister Agnes "Nell" Naughton, who passed away last evening and is watching the action from the comfort of the afterlife. Well, Nell, I suppose we can only hope that it's as glorious there as it is here today in Croke Park, where the conditions are ideal for ground hurling.'

The All-Ireland also presents the chance for us all to enjoy our indigenous sports in a whirlwind of Marty's almost super-natural grasp of another precious national phenomenon – GAA hyperbole: 'Today we will watch The Greatest Game In The World played in the glorious environs of Croke Park, probably The Most Sensational Stadium In The Whole Of The Solar System. And on this special day, we enjoy the honour of seeing Henry Shefflin – KING HENRY! The Greatest Irish Man Ever To Have Held A Stick – line out for The Cats, the greatest team of hurlers since Adam and Eve picked the apple off the tree, marshalled by Brian Cody, probably a tactician and motivator on a par with Alexander the Great. And all this takes place in Éireann, kingdom of The Gael, surely The Best Small Country In The World In Which To Overestimate One's Own Significance In The Grand Scheme Of Things.'

As sure as it unites though, sport can divide, and we are a nation of tribes, after all. So to give you a fuller flavour of these often subtle demarcation lines, I've asked five of my friends – whose names, and indeed very existence, I have disguised here because this gets fierce touchy – to write a little about their own tribe and what makes them so special.

Barney – Football

I think Gaelic football is the true sport of the Irish heart. I mean, what could be more Irish than doing something at a level that's just below professional? And Gaelic is a manly sport. Even the ladies have balls of steel. Tell me this – could Wayne Rooney take a belt of a shoulder? Could Luis Suárez sink ten pints and play full forward in a Junior C league match the following morning? They're not men. They're only in it for the money! And d'you think they'd be willing to do it week in week out, with only their mammy washing their togs and a job as an insurance salesperson at the end of it? Would they fuck! Hurling? Hurling is good too, but it's a bit too wristy for my liking. Don't talk to me about rugby or cricket, though. If I wanted to act like a Protestant I'd dress up as Harry Potter!

Ultan – Rugby

I sometimes look at boggers who play rugby and I can only marvel at the way a sport can transform men who would otherwise be working as, I dunno, tractor-repair men, and who are now, thanks to rugby, lording it as professional superheroes on a European stage. No offence to the other codes, but I think you're going to see rugby union emerge as the primary sport in Ireland in the years to come and that can only be a good thing, for literacy levels in general and for people of all shapes and sizes and from all backgrounds who want to enjoy a real sport – pacey solicitors; tall, thin barristers; even fat, dumpy district judges.

Fionnuala – Camogie

Sometimes I love camogie so much I think I'll bursht! Camogie's my whole life. What I love moesht about camogie is 'tis MAD FASHT! The fashtest field sport in the world, *didoo know that? 'Magine tirty cheetahs chasing a rat round a galley kitchen ... SAVAGE QUICK! People say 'tis dangerous. 'Tis not dangerous!!! Jusht shtick ur nose into d'other wan's armpits. And pull hard! Pull like you're in Coppers! Up Tipp!*

Dan – Couch-potato Sports Whore

I watch everything, really. My ideal Saturday I spend in my apartment, watching Sky Score Centre on the telly surrounded by two laptop screens, an iPad and my phone. I'll generally have around five different streams open – live football, horse racing, Formula One, darts – I follow them all – athletics, baseball, basketball, martial arts. It really doesn't matter. If I saw two tramps fighting on the street, I'd probably crack open a few cans and watch it, to be honest. Sport is just everything ... And nothing, in a way ...

Oh Jesus Christ, my life is a meaningless void.

Helen – Soccer

They say Gah's the sport of the people. It is in me hoop. Gah's only for Blueshirt bog monkeys and people who clean their noses with the backs of their hands. Football is the true sport of the working classes. It's a street game, see. Pelé kicked a rolled-up sock stuffed with rags around the streets of Bauru. Gilesy did the same in Ormond Square, in his bare feet. Even Eamon Dunphy started out as a young pup, roaming the backstreets of Drumcondra, randomly stoking up controversy. To be fair, what could be more working class than dreaming you might one day cruise the streets of London in a yellow Maserati, throwing cash out through the sunroof? It's

165

a tough time for football, all the same. People like Sepp Blatter have disgraced the game. Football, at its most beautiful, is a simple thing. Effortless almost. If you've seen Messi or Georgie Best or Terry Phelan in action, you'll know what I mean. You just have to keep the ball. Simple. Not lose it, like. Don't give the ball away. You have to hold on to the ball. Are you with me? That's why Ireland are shite right now. Most of them couldn't hold on to rabies if you injected it into their feet.

**When John Lennon sang
'imagine no possessions',
he was talking about being
an Irish footballer.**

Fitness

For centuries Irish people didn't have to worry unduly about their weight. Whether we were yanking calves out of cows, desperately clambering up the sides of ocean liners or simply running away from the TV-licence inspector, we always managed to keep fit and trim. These days, however, a new plague is stalking the land. Thanks to diets with Willy Wonka levels of sugar and a sedentary lifestyle bordering on the glacial, the Irish population seems to be on a one-way train to Obie-City. Some of the anecdotal evidence is shocking. Up to 64 per cent of babies born in Ireland are now Pounders (see chapter 13) and have a 100 per cent chance of suffering from obesity in later life (mainly because they're already obese within the first trimester). One schoolchild in rural Wexford had become so overweight over the course of the summer holidays, the school principal had to apply for planning permission to erect a huge corrugated outhouse where he sat out the rest of the term groaning and sweating like Jabba the Hutt.

To counteract all this, we've had to concoct new and faintly ridiculous ways to keep the national weighing scales from exploding under the immensity of our collective buttocks. The gym is often the first port of call.

Gymlife

For super-fit athletes-in-training, gyms are very functional spaces and eminently practical in a country where sideways rain can make training outdoors lethal. For most casual users (i.e. the rest of us), however, gyms are horrendous amphitheatres of self-torture filled with stale air, bad techno and thin fuckers. Sure, in January, you'll hit the mats with a great sense of optimistic enthusiasm. On day one, you'll carefully stretch out every muscle and tendon before the workout for fear of injury. You'll hydrate adequately, probably with something isotonic, whatever the hell that is. You'll build up a sweat slowly and find your rhythm. By day three you may push it out until you start to feel 'the burn'. You're getting places.

By mid-February, you may even have established some semblance of a routine – necking quinoa and water biscuits for lunch, keeping a diary of each session, tracking yards gained and pounds lost to an imagined soundtrack from *Rocky*, even running up and down steps and shouting 'Adrian!'

Unfortunately, the wheels soon come off. The excuses will start – pulled hamstring, bad traffic, slept in, Granny died again – and you'll slack off slowly. A missed day turns into a missed month. By March, and for the rest of the year, the only thing left exercising will be the direct debit for your membership fee, consistently working its way out of your bank account like a disciplined East German weightlifter. The very thought of the gym will be such a source of shame and personal failure, you promise yourself to never EVER join again. Until next January, that is, when the whole inevitable cycle begins again.

However, there is a more traditional route . . .

GAA Winter Training

GAA winter training often starts around 2 January and is an ideal New Year's regime for all the participants who are so full of Guinness and Christmas turkey they could easily be encased in filo pastry and sold off as artisan pies.

The schedule goes something like this:

5.00 a.m. Coach and selectors gather in the dressing rooms to load up a tractor with balls, bibs, cones, tyres, hatchets, lengths of Wavin pipe, barbed wire, etc.

5.30 a.m. Coaching staff burst into each player's bedroom in order of age, waking them from their slumber using foghorns, dragging them from their beds and forcing them to tog out immediately in front of them while jabbing them with cattle prods. Each player is manhandled outside, where the rest of his/her teammates are to be found pale and shivering, clinging to the rails of a trailer like recently rescued fishermen.

6.00 a.m. The team is driven to a local beach with Tina Turner's 'Simply The Best' blaring on the tractor's sound system. On the shore, they are fed a breakfast of plain white bread and undiluted pineapple MiWadi.

6.10 a.m. Warm up. Players do twenty lengths of the beach en masse. Normally, this will get most of the projectile vomiting out of the way. On average, two to three cruciate ligaments will rupture during this period.

6.30 a.m. Break. Motivational speech from the parish priest/former GAA Dual All Star.

6.55 a.m. Tractor-tyre relay. Players are strapped by the waist to large tractor tyres using baling twine and forced to pull them along the sand while doing hand-passing drills. For more experienced players, the tyres remain attached to the tractors. This goes on for approximately two episodes of *Up for the Match*.

8.35 a.m. Break – hang sangwiches, tae, shot of vomiting.

9.00 a.m. In a team-bonding exercise, three dispensable fringe players, including the sub goalie, are set on fire using red diesel. The rest of the panel has to work together to successfully lead their burning colleagues into the sea before they pass away.

9.30 a.m. Weights. In order to improve core strength and muscle tone after the Christmas excess, players are invited to lift an assortment of novelty weights, e.g. a dead goat, bales of hay and a Ford Escort Mark II (to represent the weight of expectation in the parish concerning this year's championship).

10.00 a.m. The Hill of Carvery. In this final event, participants are driven to a local hill/mountain. The aim here is for them to climb the mountain barefoot and blindfolded guided only by the smell of cooked carvery wafting from the top. Successful players are invited to eat their fill on arrival at the summit. Unsuccessful players are left to die in the wild.

11.00 a.m. To warm down, players retire to the local pub where they proceed to get polluted and reminisce about moral victories gone by.

This routine is generally followed by a five-day lay-off/copious limping before they compete in the final rounds of last year's championship.

Chapter 13

Childhood

Now that we know a little about the country and its people, it's time to get into the nitty-gritty of the Irish life cycle. As we have seen, modern Ireland is a melting pot, a broad church of people with many interesting and varied lifestyles and ambitions. But what can we say about a 'shared experience' in contemporary Ireland? I can perhaps only address the universal by first detailing the personal. And it doesn't get more personal than this.

Colm's Memoir – Extract 1

The Big Swim

'C'mon lads. Hurry up. We've got a lot done, but there's more to do!'

I could see Seamus and Mairéad moving up ahead, gesturing for me to follow. They had been swimming for just over an hour, but it felt like weeks. And these were not normal waters.

'Lads, I think we should turn back. It looks dangerous.'

'Ah stop with your whinging, Colm. You're for ever at it.' Mairéad was wriggling her bum with a determined gusto. 'We're nearly there.'

All of a sudden, up ahead, a huge, gleaming object loomed

into view, unlike anything any of us had ever seen. It rose translucent and bulbous, like the moon over Benbulbin or a white arse in the window of a school bus.

'Jesus! There it is!' said Seamus, gasping. 'Home!' If Seamus had eyes, they would surely have widened at this point.

'Holy living shit,' Mairéad offered. 'It's palatial . . . C'mon lads – SWIM!'

Approaching from the rear, a crowd of what looked like a hundred million others swam headlong behind us. I found myself suddenly overcome by raw panic.

'Can't we please go back? We were so safe and cosy, I don't know why we ever left! We were happy, Seamus.'

'We were ejaculated, Colm. From a ball bag.' He never minced his words, that Seamus. 'We came into this world – quite literally. Our only job is to get up there first.' He was pointing towards the white yolk.

'I just don't know why you're so obsessed with coming first . . .' I said.

'Stay here if you like so,' said Mairéad. 'The last thing Ireland needs now is another miserable cunt feeling sorry for himself.'

'Ireland? We're Irish?! I thought we were French?!' This didn't suit me at all.

'Nah, we're pure Irish,' said Seamus proudly, like he was radio-advertising sausages. 'Why else do you think we've been having such good craic?'

'But, but . . .'

This was not good news. See, I had this dream of a warm, quiet life on some Mediterranean hilltop village, drinking wine, having tempestuous affairs with the local butcher's daughter, producing artisanal cheese, etc. But now this beautiful dream was coming crash-landing to the ground, to be replaced by the dawning reality of damp bungalows, Bovril and people who say butter without pronouncing the 't's.

If I was lucky.

All of a sudden, we heard a long whining sound approaching from the rear as another swimmer settled in beside us.

'How's things, folks? Nearly there, wha'!' If we had hands he surely would have shook them firmly.

'Who's this fucker now?' I thought, in the same way we all do when approached by some distant relative at a family function.

'Pádraig's my name. I was wondering if I could ask you for your vote?'

He had the sort of high-pitched, scooter-like quality to his voice that you often hear going on and on for hours at local festival openings.

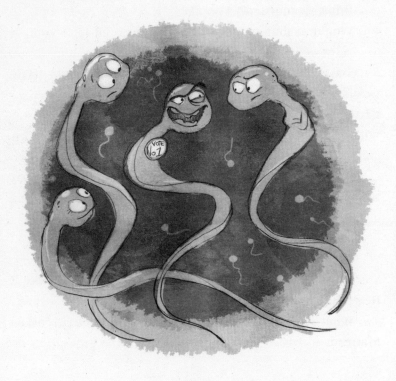

'Ask for our what?' said Mairéad, annoyed by this sudden distraction.

'Lookit, the other lads back there are putting me forward to represent them when we get up there,' he said, gesturing towards the egg, which was even closer now. 'And I'm out canvassing for your vote.'

'Canvassing? It's far from canvassing we were reared!' said Mairéad. 'What's in it for us anyway?'

Pádraig cleared his throat. 'Well, I can make you a fervent promise – a covenant if you will – to represent your best interests on our shared journey through the uterus.'

'What's a uterus?' I asked.

Pádraig ignored me. 'The message I have been receiving on the doorsteps is that all sperm want equal representation, going forward. And I'm the man with the plan!'

'What's a doorstep?' I persisted.

'Would ya shut up, Colm,' said Seamus.

Pádraig continued. 'All I'm asking is that you let me speak for you on arrival, to represent, as I have previously stated, your best interests. And sure we'll have a few scoops after, wha'?!' If he had elbows, he would surely have poked me with one of them.

'I'm not so sure—'

Now, there's an ancient Irish saying that 'all sperm are slippery', but I could tell straight away that we were entering a whole new level of slipperiness with this little prick.

Seamus and Mairéad seemed less suspicious.

'Can you give us a minute to confer?'

'Oh sure, work away. I'll be swimming along over here.' He whistled as he left.

'What do ye think lads, is it worth giving him a go?' asked Mairéad.

'He seems reliable,' said Seamus. 'I liked the stuff about sharing and going forward and promises and all that. Decent skin, I reckon.'

'Hang on a minute . . .' I couldn't believe my ears. 'Won't this jackass just get to the egg first and leave us all behi—'

'But he said he'd look after us, Colm,' pointed out Mairéad.

'Yeah, don't be so cynical. You heard him – he's the man with the plan!' Seamus boomed.

At that moment I experienced what I can only describe as a spiritual event. You know the way they say that your life flashes in front of your eyes just before you die? Well, in this case, the entire collective memory of my Irish DNA played out in front of me like a Christmas special of *Reeling in the Years*.

I saw a landlord evicting a family of starving farmers. I saw a priest leading a child away by the hand. I saw the board of Anglo Irish Bank gyrating on barstools made from the foreskins of whales. I saw Johnny Logan composing thoughtfully at a piano. I saw an e-voting machine gathering dust. I saw Sally O'Brien and the way she might look at you. I saw Darby O'Gill. I saw the Little People. I saw the weather forecast for the following Saturday.

And then I inhaled, gathering in every molecule of air that I possibly could – remarkable given that I had no nose, mouth, throat or lungs – and I roared: 'ENOOOOOOUUUUUUUGH!!!'

Then there was silence.

Every other sperm stopped in its tracks and a peculiar atmosphere settled over the entire uterus. All at once, I found myself in the possession of a fierce, primal energy. You know the way you'd feel after three pints? I left Seamus, Mairéad and the slippery fucker for dead. I shook my spermy little butt and propelled myself forwards like I was Michelle Smith. Then, before I knew it, I was home.

As I burrowed head first into the egg, I was enveloped by a new sort of quietness and serenity, a heightened feeling of pampered safety you rarely experience outside of a hotel lodge and spa. Then, I heard one of the most gorgeous sounds to have ever graced my ears.

'Welcome,' it whispered. 'Welcome to Egg.' These words reverberated around for a while. It's hard to do justice to the beauty of it but it sounded a bit like Miriam O'Callaghan.

'Th . . . thanks . . . Who are you?'

'I'm your feminine side, Colm.'

'Feminine side? What's that when it's at home?'

'You see, I've been repressed in Irish men for many centuries but I'm getting a bit of a fair go these days, what with the feminist revolution, legally enforceable EU directives and all that. You'll need to start listening to me from now on.'

'How so?'

'I'm here to help you with a range of things that won't come naturally to you – multitasking, rational thinking, displaying humility, not starting wars, to name but four.'

'Looks like I'll need all the help I can get!' I joked.

'You have no idea.'

Everything about this new side of me made me feel calm and relaxed.

'Well, it's wonderful to meet you, feminine side. I look forward to a fruitful partnership, going forward.'

'Me too. Oh, and don't use those words – going forward. Don't be a fucking spanner, Colm.'

'Okey-dokey.'

And, to be honest, that is all I can fully remember about my conception.

Bonnie Babies

Every year, across Ireland, tens of thousands of beautiful little Irish babies are born. These little creatures represent the future of our fine country and before they've even had time to do their first wee, they each owe around thirty thousand euros to various secured and unsecured international creditors. Give or take. This is known as original sin and is a concept inherited from Catholicism, whereby every innocent, newborn child is saddled with the huge cost of what a few idiots did in the Garden of Eden (aka the Celtic Tiger).

It's no wonder they cry so much.

They say that every baby is born unique, with their own set of quirks and melange of genetic traits. But if this is true, then why is it that there are only four types of baby in Ireland?

What do you mean you haven't noticed?

In any pram, crèche or bonnie-baby competition across the land (and you can check this if you don't believe me) every single baby up to six months old falls into one of only four categories.

Category A: The Pounder

The Pounder is a big butterball of a baby, usually weighing in at between twelve and fourteen stone. Pounders come packed with more folds than the Galtee Mountains, more chins than Alfred Hitchcock and they have been known to have buttocks that go on for furlongs. One Pounder born in Athlone in 2013 became world famous after Commander Hadfield started tweeting pictures of her from space. These babies are often greeted positively by the community – 'Isn't she a fine size?' – but, in truth, they can be a massive strain on the resources of their parents, the emergency services and the electricity grid.

Some Pounders are born so unwieldy, they have to be air-lifted back home by search-and-rescue professionals, rolled up the driveway on logs employing the same technique the Egyptians used to build the Pyramids, before being installed in the garden on giant wooden stilts where they are fed with hoses by their exhausted parents. And the mother is bound to be exhausted. Giving birth to a Pounder is said to be, pound for pound, the physical equivalent to squeezing out an adult walrus. Pounders are often referred to as 'stout children'.

Category B: The Wayne Rooney

Mysteriously, about 35 per cent of Irish babies arrive into the world looking exactly like pre-hair-exten-sion-surgery Wayne Rooney. Look into any random pram on the street and I guarantee you a tiny Wayne Rooney in a bonnet will be staring right back. Of course it is a national tragedy and, indeed, a mystery, that our success producing Wayne Rooney babies hasn't translated into any recent success in international football.

Category C: Premature Yoda Babies

Literally born before their time, these lads are. And wise beyond their years too. Premature Yoda Babies are often born a bit shrivelled and have to be kept in an incubator. It is here that they begin plotting ways to exact revenge on their parents and the medical profession for forcing them into an early checkout from the womb. Many PYBs end up getting jobs in the Central Bank, such is their wisdom and ability to predict future behaviour. But some of them, those who can't get past the early birth thing, can end up as supervillains with underground lairs/working for tobacco companies. They tend not to be very good craic.

Category D: The Hairy Baby

Hairy babies are very common in Ireland and some of our most prized personalities were born this way, e.g. Brendan Grace, Doctor James Reilly and anybody who has ever worked in a trade union. With a Hairy Baby, it can often take up to six months to figure out which side of the head you are supposed to be looking at. Once this confusing initial period has passed, the Hairy Baby will soon realize they are indeed very lucky to be born in Ireland. They will already have a head start in the world of folk music, they will be warmer in the winter and they are likely to pick up a good bit of work as extras on *Game of Thrones*.

Chapter 14

Education

For most people, childhood is a wonderfully innocent and happy time. When you're young the days seem to stretch on like years. At age four, turning twelve seems aeons away. It's easy to forget it, but there are things you can get away with as a child that become somehow frowned upon as you get older.

These include:

- Soiling yourself
- Leaping on to your parents' bed at 6 a.m. and kicking your father square in the face
- Turning light switches off and on and off and on and off again
- Walking around the house naked while shouting

In Ireland we've had a long history of treating children and their mothers with all the dignity of a minor rodent infestation – e.g. hiding them away in industrial schools, laying out poison for them, hitting them over the head with shovels – but things have improved markedly in recent decades. It's fair to say that the average middle-class Irish child enjoys a lifestyle not unlike that of a touring Venetian prince from the fifteenth century – being driven around everywhere in a small chariot, having a never-ending calendar of society parties as well as occasional recurrences of gout.

Like many Irish children of my generation, I enjoyed an egalitarian community education, which was more or less free, where every student was treated well and encouraged to progress all the way to college. Our teachers didn't know it at the time, but with their ambition for us, they were essentially destroying lucrative opportunities in international misery literature, particularly in the American market. All this amounts to a gross injustice perpetrated on people of my generation. Our predecessors enjoyed huge financial windfalls on the back of books like *Angela's Ashes* and films like *My Left Foot*. Even Peig drove a Beemer in the end. Bar a few freezing afternoons watching *Bosco*, most of us really don't have a whole lot to complain about. Indeed, it's only a matter of time before the children of the eighties, nineties and beyond bring a class action against the Irish education system, so we might recoup all those future royalties, film-option deals, chat-show appearance fees, etc. Here's how it could have been.

Colm's Memoir – Extract 2

National(ism) School

West Cork, 1980s – rain, destitution, misery, more rain . . . There was a lingering sense of famine that still stalked the land, even though it had been over a century now since the Great Potato Crash. There was a feeling in the air that every townland in rural Ireland was populated by ghosts, wandering the back roads, trapped for ever inside some perpetually unspooling vortex of misery and pain. The land itself seemed to object to the very presence of the people trying to leech a living off it, in the burgeoning supermarkets, the children's boutiques and the small factories where they made the Pretty Polly tights. The hollow trees emerged from the earth like black, bony claws. The dark spectres of churning SodaStreams threw their shadows across the teabag-stained lino of perpetually freezing kitchens.

Did I mention it was raining?

I don't know where I was born exactly. I was once told that I floated into Bantry Bay in a fish box . . . All I know for sure is that for the first ten years of my life I lived in a coalshed at the bottom of a churchyard, which I shared with between ten and forty other children. None of us had any idea how we got there. It was cold, damp, mucky, wet, soft, soggy, slippery, mouldy and you couldn't move for cut knees and whooping cough. In the evenings, the parish priest would drag us all out by the hair and one of the town drunks would hit us with spoons for the amusement of passing dignitaries. If we were lucky. We had no clothes to speak of, only old rags we had found round the back of a TB hospital in the bad winter of 1983. I had a pair of dungarees I hid from the others and used to wear them on Christmas Day.

Sanitation was poor. We all shared a latrine that we dug out of the soil with our hands only a few feet away from where we slept. It was full of beetles and rats and wasps and the discarded shoes of a thousand altar boys. In the end, it got blocked up and for most of 1984 we had to shit in a coffin. In the rain.

In the evenings the whole town would gather round a small black-and-white portable telly watching rerun marathons of *MacGyver*. Oh, the sport and *spraoi* we would have, in the fierce battle for the front-row seats! People were pulled and dragged and sat on, in a violent rush to get the best view. In the end we'd all sit watching it in a huge pile of bodies, those at the bottom gasping for breath. When *MacGyver* ended, we'd watch *Cagney and Lacey* or *Jake and the Fatman*. One Saturday, ten people were squashed to death trying to watch *Sports Stadium*.

When it wasn't bucketing down, we were being split open by thin shards of sleet a mile long and when the wind wasn't ripping the very skin from our cheekbones we were being pummelled by hailstones the size of badgers. I swear to God, the first time I ever saw sunshine was on *Baywatch*.

Our school, a former asylum that stood grey and imposing on the side of a hill, was basically Guantanamo Bay with tin whistles. Our teacher, a furious little Blueshirt with chronic piles, would spend whole mornings goading us and poking us with a hurl just to pass the time. When he wasn't torturing us with physical violence, he would unleash great, unrelenting waves of psychological abuse upon us, primarily around the themes of masturbation/blindness/the civil war. He hated Michael Jackson's 'Billie Jean' with a passion.

We learnt nothing of any real use. He taught us Latin for the craic. He spent much of his time standing at the head of the classroom, with eyes slammed shut, speaking in tongues about Cromwell's crimes against Ireland, frothing at the mouth about the tyranny of British oppression, spewing rancid bile *as Gaeilge* about fuck-knows-what. In the afternoons, he would pull off his putrefying socks and cut his toenails in front of us using blunt scissors, shrapnel flying around the classroom, every little snip a small assassination attempt. We all took to wearing helmets. In the rain.

I sat next to a young lad called Chris who seemed to do nothing but eat eggs. For small break, he ate a hard-boiled egg. For lunch, an egg sandwich. After school, he'd knock back a raw egg, as a snack. In art class, he constantly drew impressionistic vistas around the theme of eggs: an egg driving a tractor, Adolf Hitler giving a speech to a stadium full of eggs and he even created surreal Dalí-inspired renderings of the Humpty Dumpty story. To top all this, he farted more or less constantly. From morning prayers to the final bell, his eggy emissions would linger in the air like Agent Orange.

Looking back on it now, I suppose it would be easy to be bitter about it all. To hold a grudge. But we pulled ourselves out of it, in the end. If you can for one minute look beyond the repression, the destitution, the malnutrition, the abandonment, the corruption – both moral and institutional – the two channels of television and the storage heating . . . I suppose, at the end of the day, we survived. We all eventually moved on to good jobs in software engineering, hedge-fund management and the law (Chris became a clinical embryologist). Most, if not all of us, are in massive negative equity.

A Guide to Communionism

We've all heard the phrase 'Sure, she's still got her Communion money'. This means that the subject is either admirably astute or perishing mean, depending on your perspective. In Ireland, your first introduction to aggressive capitalism occurs early, under a system known as communionism. Under communionist economics, a child is presented with an early financial windfall from relatives and is then expected to have the cop-on to use it wisely. The true tragedy is that these poorly advised cherubs don't realize the potential of the opportunity before them and often blow everything they've accumulated on a single substantial capital investment, like a bike, which loses half its value the minute you wheel it out of the shop.

So, to help these young angels avoid some of the common

pitfalls inherent in the system, here is a short financial guide to communionism.

1. Look the Part

For girls, the white dress, gloves, flowers and veil are par for the course. The most important accoutrement, however, is a generously dimensioned sequinned purse. This may look like the perfect addition to the oh-my-God-isn't-she-adorable ensemble, but it's really a cute little brown envelope waiting to be filled. Play your cards right and this thing will be bursting with hard cash by the time lunch is done and Uncle Fachtna is projectile-vomiting into the hotel jacuzzi. It is also, handily enough, the perfect size to carry a credit-card machine.

If you're a little boy, it's best to go the full Oliver Twist on it. Even though your parents probably had to remortgage the house to buy your suit, you should pull your pockets out, ruffle up your hair, daub your cheeks with shoe polish and brush up on your cockney. A little patch of runny snot around the nostril area will also help. The trick, then, is to wander around the congregation, slipping into family photos like some sort of Victorian ghost. Grannies, grandaunts and kindly uncles of other children will likely shower you with coins and notes, just to make you go away. It is thought that you can increase your initial pool of cash by up to 40 per cent using this simple technique. Crashing other children's Communions should not be ruled out either. Don't be afraid to grow your business.

2. Learn To Save and Invest

It is vital that you understand the fundamentals of compound interest as soon as possible. Granted, you may still be struggling with basic arithmetic at this age, but the clever ones, the little Smurfits and O'Briens and Trumps, will know that lump sums invested when you're seven can multiply exponentially if distributed in the proper manner. Of course, a basic understanding of the markets will be necessary in order to spread your risk and reap the full benefit. So a *Financial Times* subscription should be on the list for Santa this year. More advanced children might consider a simple Ponzi scheme among classmates.

3. Hands Off, Parents!

The most nefarious threat to a good communionist outcome is the meddling of do-goody parents. Firstly, they will blow extraordinary amounts of money on dresses, jewellery, flowers, food, Hummers, discos, balls, bad clowns and bouncy castles, pretending it is all for your benefit. Make no mistake; it is not. They only wish to look better in the eyes of their peers, the saps. Secondly, like the government, they will do whatever they can to get their hands on your cash. Having promised you the sun, moon and stars they will patronizingly offer to 'keep the money safe, darling'. This should never be allowed. The money will inevitably be siphoned off to pay for current expenditure like schoolbooks, heating or the Universal Social Charge. Worse still, they may even attempt to redistribute it among your other siblings. This is communism, not communionism, and know this: it will only end in tyranny. If these parents had any sense, they would leave well alone and wait for the money to grow and grow and grow until a fortune has accumulated, a fortune which, if they play their cards right, will, one day, trickle down to them in old age.

The Leaving

It was my intention here to write about the teenage years and puberty but after only ten minutes' work I found myself rocking back and forth in the corner of the room, crying, looking to the ceiling. I have clearly been blocking out personal memories of this time, but suffice it to say, the whole experience is a bit like that film *The Fly*, when Jeff Goldblum mutates into a disgusting half-man, half-insect – he sheds layers and layers of weird oily skin, hair sprouts out from his back, he grows wings and a series of mortifying and involuntary bodily emissions take place in situations that couldn't possibly be more public.

This is all only mildly less traumatic than the Leaving Certificate.

For those of you who don't know it, the Leaving is a series of final secondary-school exams devised to work like a particularly sick and twisted Japanese TV game show, which challenges you to remember every single pointless fact in the history of the world in under two hours and on punishment of death. To compound the underlying theme of psychological torture, these exams are timetabled every year for the beginning of June, a mysterious period in the Irish meteorological calendar whereby scorching Mediterranean weather is guaranteed across all of the country.

The media, of course, loses its mind. On the one hand, you have weighty editorials expressing concern about the mental health of our young people and the stress they are being put under, yet on the other, they'll have exam supplements the size of the *Collins English Dictionary* packed to the rafters with exam tips, fad diets to improve your mental capacity and adverts for sun-holiday packages in Magaluf. Of course, after a few days of feigned collective concern and sympathy, everyone totally forgets about the students and fecks off to the beach.

In truth, these poor youngsters need to take a step back and remember a simple, salient fact: the Leaving Cert doesn't really matter that much in the grand scheme of things. In Ireland, it's who you're related to that really counts.

What do we have to show for all the revision and cramming and grind in the end? Once they've vomited all that knowledge on to the page and got their CAO place, the worried and emaciated students will spend the next four to twelve years of university doing everything within their power to obliterate every single brain cell in their craniums.

Really, there is only one thing they can truly look forward to holding on to after this trying and testing period.

The Leaving Cert anxiety dream . . .

The Classic

In the classic Leaving Cert anxiety dream, it is the day of English Paper 1 and you wake up in a cold sweat to find you have done absolutely no study. You glance at your phone and you see it's 4.30 p.m.

You wake in your bed screaming.

The Dentalist

A less common one this; you are sitting in the exam hall working through Honours Maths Paper 1 and things are going swimmingly. You're even a bit ahead of schedule. As you are about to solve yet another equation with apparent ease, you notice one of your teeth plopping out on to the graph paper below. It is soon followed by a second tooth, a molar, and shortly after, a third. Soon enough, your teeth begin to cascade on to the page below like Scrabble tiles, one after the other. In panic, you start to try to count them. 1, 2, 5, 16 . . . You recoil in horror as you realize you have completely forgotten how to count. You grab for your calculator to see if it can help, but the battery is dead. You are now sitting there, all gummy and panicked, looking around at all your classmates as they hand in their papers early and skip out the door towards an awaiting ice-cream van. You brush the teeth away from the desk and begin to try working on the equation again but notice that you've not got the pencil any more, you're holding a giant rubber chicken.

You wake in a cold sweat, screaming and biting your spouse's ankle.

The David Lynch

It is the morning of the Geography paper and you are lying in bed, preparing to get up. You feel confident. You have revised well for this. You're ready. As you attempt to rise, you realize that you can't move any of your limbs. You are completely paralysed. You try to cry out for help but you can't even exercise your vocal cords. Suddenly, a red curtain is pulled across the room, the lights go down and you hear the sound of lounge jazz. The door of the room opens and your eyes widen as you see novelty country-and-western entertainer Richie Kavanagh, midget-sized and with a horrifying grimace on his face, tiptoe across the room in time with the music. Richie suddenly begins talking backwards as the jazz shuffle continues. After an excruciating minute of weirdness, your bed and the whole room begin to drift up and come apart in space and time. You are now left floating in an eerie star-filled blackness, Richie

193

levitating above you, still talking backwards. Suddenly he lurches down towards you like a dragon, rushing towards your face. You wake screaming and roaring.

Relieved to be able to feel your limbs again, and to be out of the nightmare, you get up and reach down to put on your slippers. Richie Kavanagh, grimacing ever still, slides out suddenly from under the bed and grabs you by the legs to pull you under.

You wake screaming and roaring.

The Nightmare Scenario

You actually do pretty well in your Leaving Cert, getting a total of 475 points, and go through the college years happily, before entering the workplace. Once set up in a job, you gradually submit to a life of repetition and drudgery, settling for a career you never quite dreamed about, but which pays well. You have 2.5 children, take 1.75 holidays a year and buy a house in Dublin's commuter belt.

You never wake up.

Chapter 15

Love and Marriage

The history of sex in Ireland is long and complex and gets a bit sweaty, but thankfully it can be neatly summed up in one sentence. Everyone clearly kept having lots of it, because we're all still here.

Sex was officially banned outside marriage in Ireland until 1987 and even then could only take place under a strict set of conditions: it had to be a Friday night, directly after *The Late Late Show* and never went on for longer than three minutes and forty-two seconds. It was also, generally, supervised by a member of the clergy.

If we jump back to Ireland in the 1960s, things were very different to today. The country at the time was culturally light years removed from the free love of the American counterculture, where 'there was music in the cafés at night and revolution in the air'. In Catholic Ireland by contrast, there was Brendan Bowyer in the dance hall and a serious smell of cowshit in the air. Such was the brute force of their pent-up and repressed sexual passions, Irish women were throwing their knickers at Bowyer at an awful rate. It's hard to imagine now the depths of repression required to move you to take off your *actual* pants in a crowded public space and throw them at a man with a microphone, but this was the sad reality of the era.

The Ten Commandments for Irish Women in 1970

1 You shalt not keep your job if you get married.

2 You shalt not sit on a jury.

3 You shalt not take the contraceptive pill.

4 You shalt not drink a pint in a pub.

5 Okay, you can sit in the snug, but only for the Women's Christmas.

6 You shalt not refuse to have sex with your husband.

7 You shalt not get equal pay for doing the same work as a man.

8 You shalt sit down and shut up, you silly woman.

9 You shalt cover up those knees.

10 You shalt give that glass ceiling a good aul' clean, seeing as you're up there under it.

Romantic Ireland

Nowadays, thankfully, we live in a far healthier sexual culture (apart from all the STDs, that is). It helps that many people, the world over, consider the Irish to be a nation of romantics. If our representation in de fillums is to be believed, they all imagine us leppin' over stone walls with a rose between our teeth, wide-eyed and passionate, as we elope hand in hand across moonlit fields, singing out the poetry of W. B. Yeats as our true love runs, nay, frolics, by our side (with a cute little puppy poking its head out of a top pocket, probably).

These people have clearly never walked into a teenage disco in Tullamore.

From what I remember of them, Irish teenage discos had a general atmosphere not unlike a Studio 54 orgy, with hundreds of bodies in various stages of arousal, mortification and crisis pregnancy, strewn across an indoor sports hall. This was all inevitably accompanied by a soundtrack of bad pop music and the gasps of horrified school supervisors, who would have no option but to move, ashen-faced, among the revellers, occasionally prising them apart like undercooked mussels. You see, matters of the heart in Ireland were, and often still are, settled in a surprisingly straightforward fashion.

First Base

The Shift describes the accepted 'unit' of kissing and groping, and is traditionally the Irish person's first introduction to the world of physical intimacy. The Shift is generally a prearranged act at a disco or behind some building (any shed or handball alley will do), which is well out of the watchful gaze of any prudish adults but generally on view to all your friends, who will often sit around rating the act on Twitter. For the most part, The Shift will be organized by a third party, who will pose the question 'Will you shift my friend?' before pointing at the potential shiftee, who will be standing there, looking directly into the ground, praying for it to open up and deliver them to some other location along the quantum field. In many ways, this is just a slightly more innocent version of the Point-Accept-Copulate system of romantic engagement that has been a staple of Irish romantic life for generations.

Incidentally, nobody is quite sure where the phrase 'The

Shift' originated, but it probably has something to do with the fact that it is a fairly effective way to move disease quickly around a community.

Second Base

Things get a bit more involved at second base, or as Irish people refer to it, 'wearing the face off someone'. In this prolonged and fairly disgusting activity, couples perform an act of extended resuscitation on one another for hours and hours and hours and sometimes days on end, becoming attached in a manner not unlike the face-hugging scene from *Alien*. It is, in essence, a sort of consensual hygiene apocalypse where both parties are often afraid to pull away, for fear of total peer ostracization. After a few hours of wearing the face off someone, you are inevitably forced to release your limpet-like grip in order to avoid asphyxiation. This detachment must be done slowly and carefully, however, to ward against an episode of the bends, which would probably require a decompression procedure in hospital. Once separated, both retire, dehydrated and cross-eyed no doubt, to hoover up fizzy drinks in silence in a chipper, like two dead-eyed Vietnam vets on some San Francisco park bench.

Home Run

Although there is a third base in Ireland known as 'dropping the hand', an act which generally happens around Junior Cert results night, I am not going to get into it here (mainly because my mother will be reading this book). The home-run stage in Ireland is generally referred to as The Ride. The Ride will often take place for the first time in Magaluf or some other sun-drenched shitbox, during the summer after the Leaving Cert, although most people will lie and pretend it happened far sooner. This is a time of great exploration for young people, freed from the shackles of school, and it is equally a time of deep and unremitting horror for their parents, who will often stay awake for days on end, huddled in fear around a laptop screen, as they unsuccessfully try to stalk them on Facebook.

It should be said, for balance, that more sensible kids, e.g. those raised with a moral compass, will often lose their virginity later on during the college years, at which stage it will almost inevitably involve at least one nurse.

Dating

As people move on in life, they inevitably start to think about settling down. One of the first things you need in order to achieve this is another human being, someone to love and share the adventure of life with. Or else a dog.

For many generations, Irish people sought out companionship by engaging in an activity called 'courting', which is a word used to describe a prolonged period of not touching someone before a massively uncomfortable proposal of marriage. Courting activity generally involved around half the parish tagging along as chaperones and Éamon de Valera had to personally review each 'courting' himself, before a second date would be approved.

After this time, and once contraception became legal, 73.4 per cent of young single Irish people followed the formula of meeting blind drunk in a bad nightclub and falling into bed together, before figuring out that they were actually strangely compatible and getting hitched a few years later.

Nowadays, thankfully, this is considered a bit common and uncouth. In contemporary Ireland lonely hearts often begin the search for true love in the safe and welcoming environment of the online world, where all the barriers are lifted to a rich new world of potential partners across all sections of society and indeed across different continents (not to mention all the dangerous weirdos out there).

It is an arena fraught with misdirection, however, as the following examples from Tinder are testament. Things aren't always what they seem.

Tinder Profile
Colin, 38
3 miles away

My name is Colin. I am a 38-year-old professional man from the Skerries area and I am looking for someone to share the rest of my life with. No pressure! ;) I enjoy golf, rugby and foreign travel and I am passionate about my work as a barrister. No time-wasters need apply!

Reality
Colin, 43
3 miles away

My name is Colin. I am actually 43, not 38, and I'm one of the biggest clowns you will ever meet. I say I want to share my life with you, but in reality, all I want is a nice young blonde thing to dangle on my arm at the weddings of other barristers, many of whom, I should add, because I always speak legalistically with many sub-clauses, are even bigger tossers than I am. You'll probably like me on the first few dates, because I'm used to putting forward a convincing case, but in time you will come to hate me with the same sort of intense, instinctive repulsion you felt after watching that online video of the ISIS beheading you were repeatedly told not to watch, but did anyway.

Tinder Profile
Denise, 35
5 miles away

My name is Denise! Hola! I am just back from a year living in Barcelona and I'm looking for a bit of excitement in my life. My hobbies include windsurfing, the music of Jack Johnson and a glass of wine every now and again. My ideal date is a picnic on a cliff-top overlooking the Atlantic Ocean, followed by a long walk on the beach and maybe even more! Adiós! xxx

Reality
Denise, 35
5 miles away

Speaking Spanish in fits and starts, although irritating enough on its own, is only one in a long list of things which will make you actively hate me within a month of our

relationship starting. In fact, it will soon emerge that I have no internal monologue whatsoever, which will become a bit wearing once I begin criticizing absolutely everything you do, right as you do it, in front of your friends, colleagues and your own mother. You will also soon come to despise that tattoo of the rare New Zealand mountain bird on my left ankle. Funnily enough, that tattoo will also be the first thing to catch your eye when you walk in on me having sex with your cousin at that family christening in Thurles in a few weeks' time.

Tinder Profile
Brendan, 64
5 miles away

My name is Brendan. I want a woman. Good luck now.

Reality
Brendan, 64
5 miles away

My name is Brendan and I am unique in that I am the only person on this app who has told the truth on his profile page. The thing is, I'm a fairly simple man who lives at home on a farm. I'm actually reliable, honest and a kind, loving person, who has a surprising passion for landscape painting (I am completely self-taught). Mad as it sounds, I have the potential to make you very happy, if you could only get beyond your stereotypical idea of an Irish bachelor farmer. Of course, you'll never find any of this out because you just swiped left, didn't you?

The Traditional Wedding

The traditional Irish wedding has fallen out of favour in recent years, but it is still known to occur from time to time. These events typically have a guest list of about five hundred people, including everyone you are related to, every single person you ever went to school with and every single person your parents have ever made eye contact with over the course of their entire lives. There will be another three or four hundred guests invited to the afters, so as to completely eliminate any risk of offence. These events are designed to make the optimum amount of cash for the absolute least amount of effort.

The day will generally progress as follows:

9 a.m. Wedding Mass, conducted by the local priest. The highlight of the Mass is the slightly risqué joke from the priest about how drunk he'll be at the reception later.

10.15 a.m. The Mass has ended, it is time to go and serve the Lord. You begin to feel as if you are serving the Lord quite quickly in fact, standing for two hours straight in the churchyard, surrounded by the headstones of departed bishops, taking GAA-style photos of every possible grouping permutation of your relations, including aunts, grandaunts, dead uncles, second cousins once removed and a few lads smoking Carrolls who were digging a grave and got pushed into a group shot by mistake.

12 noon Pints.

1 p.m. Rake of sangwiches at the hotel. These hotels are generally airport-sized, with carpet so offensively patterned it gives you the urge to vomit all over it immediately. This carpet has had the sweat of ten thousand drunk uncles repeatedly hokey pokied into it since the early 1950s and would actually cause a dangerous explosion if set alight due to friction caused by e.g. excessive rowing during 'Rock The Boat'. Because of all this, these places generally smell like your insides and the manager could badly do with a bit of help from the Brennan Brothers.

3 p.m. Pints.

4 p.m. Pints.

5 p.m. Bell for dinner.

5.45 p.m. Panic stockpiling of pints, for the meal like.

6 p.m. Starter – oxtail soup and yesterday's bread. You'll notice that the butter has a little curl in it. Nice touch that.

6.10 p.m. The dinner staff return aggressively after ten minutes with beef or salmon and enough overcooked vegetables to supply the combined forces of Boko Haram and the Lord's Resistance Army for a month. They will come back every two minutes offering 'More veg?' and catapult it on to your plate before you get a chance to accept.

6.20 p.m. Dessert – jelly and ice cream. Many guests are now suffering from third-degree heartburn. At least one uncle is heaped over the side of a chair and many people are afraid to check his pulse for fear he'll explode across the top table.

6.30 p.m. Father of the bride speaks. This speech will start in a hideously uncomfortable manner as everyone tries to discern whether he has had a stroke, is currently having a stroke or is actually making a speech. Around twenty minutes in, the speech settles into a rhythm by which time 34 per cent of the audience is beginning to nod off. The mother of the bride will generally say nothing, lost as she is inside that elaborate fascinator that rises high up into the function room, like some man-made rainforest microclimate at the Botanic Gardens.

7.30 p.m. Father of the groom speaks. After an introduction involving a series of guttural stops and what could have been a bowel movement, he settles suddenly back into his seat to bemused silence. But he doesn't really care, seeing as he's not paying for any of this.

8.30 p.m. The groom is handed the microphone and approaches his task with all the relish of a man being handed a death sentence. It doesn't help that the mother of the groom, tipsy on gin, heckles her own son. What follows is a forty-minute exercise in sweating and self-torture as he approaches the awful, horrifying moment when he has to say something emotional to the bride. The bride sits in silence for the entire event, although it has been noted many times that she and the bridesmaids look 'absolutely *stunning*'.

9.15 p.m. After around 307 awful mother-in-law jokes, the best man finally finds his rhythm when he gets an uncomfortable laugh while insinuating that the groom might be a bit of a sheep-shagger. The mother of the groom, now well beyond tipsy, commandeers the microphone to settle a few scores but is drowned out by the sound of the band leader shouting 'Teshting one-two, one-two' into his own microphone, much to everyone's relief.

9.45 p.m. Pints and night food. Sandwiches are rolled out on huge 'hang stands' and distributed to the guests who, although not that hungry, wolf them down for soakage and because they're free.

10 p.m. The band starts. If you've ever heard a cat being mangled inside a combine harvester, you've a good idea what a typical Country & Irish wedding band sounds like. A cacophony of keyboard and drum machines, an out-of-tune guitar and vocal stylings that faintly recall whooping cough, the band can often play the same song for up to five hours straight without anyone noticing. A great time will be had by all.

12 midnight The disco starts with a forty-minute loop of the 'Birdie Song', with dancing led by the priest, now as drunk as earlier threatened. Nobody really remembers what happens after that.

All in all, a great day out.

The Boutique Wedding

If the traditional wedding follows a predictable, well-worn path, then the increasingly popular boutique wedding goes to the other end of the spectrum whereby the couple tailor every single aspect of the day in order to express their own unique personalities. In general, boutique weddings tend to involve all the lavish production complexities of an Orson Welles movie (and often the associated financial success) and require the couple to reinvent the wheel at every single point of the day. This may involve creating a religion they can both agree on for the ceremony (the details of which they distribute on hand-crafted parchment scrolls before the legally binding marriage ceremony), all the way to designing their own attire, often by upcycling a personal garment, like a Communion dress or curtains with 'a personal story' attached, e.g. the bride's childhood cat Salvador used to repeatedly climb up these old curtains when she was a kid, much to the chagrin of the father of the bride. Although Salvador can't be here today (because he was hit by a bread van in 1992), his feline spirit is alive and well and, no doubt, hanging off the hem of the wedding dress as the bride gracefully approaches whatever they've installed to replace an altar.

There will inevitably be some noses out of joint over who gets an invitation to the event because it's problematic to fit more than a hundred people into a custom-fabricated igloo, which is where the ceremony takes place. Because of limited space, the couple is forced to reluctantly carpet-bomb their way through decades of tradition and the expectations of distant aunties, who are *not* impressed to be left out, instigating any number of interfamilial cold wars that are sure to linger on for many decades.

The reception will, without doubt, take place in some quirky venue in the process of active Protestant descendancy and the hipster food (generally incorporating quail) will probably be served on slates. The meal itself will be accompanied by hand-crafted favours, e.g. flowers picked by the couple on a Sardinian hilltop, pressed over many months by the exhausted wedding party in their living room and carefully arranged into glass jars, recycled from American craft-beer bottles and handblown by the groom's uncle in Waterford.

The evening music will generally contain a short break for a large-scale visual event, e.g. fireworks, the liberation of 10,000 budgies, synchronized dad-dancing. Inevitably there will be another event the next day, a barbecue probably, where, in a nod to tradition, everyone gets completely and utterly polluted drunk.

Gay Marriage

'The Day That Ireland Turned Pink' read the rather misleading *Sunday Times* headline when marriage equality was voted into law here in 2015. The truth is, thanks in large part to the farmer's tan, everybody in Ireland regularly turns pink during the summer. But the sentiment was correct. Ireland came out to the world.

It is hard to believe now, but up until the 1990s, homosexuality was illegal in Ireland. But as soon as Ireland voted to enshrine marriage equality in the Constitution, it took Fáilte Ireland all of ten minutes to launch a campaign to raise awareness of Ireland as a gay-wedding destination and attract the pink dollar. Cute hoors, like.

There was a lot of fearmongering at the time of this referendum, about what might happen if gay marriage came to pass as a legal right in Ireland. I reproduce here for posterity a leaflet that fell through my door during that difficult period.

WELL HOLY GOD!
MARCH LEAFLET

The Slippery Slope of Allowing Marriage for The Gays

Scenario 1: Farmer A and Farmer B are brothers and bachelor farmers from Kerry. Farmer A, being the eldest, is due to inherit the farm once his father goes to Heaven. What is to stop Farmer B taking Farmer A into Tralee one Saturday, getting him badly inebriated in the pub, before forcing him to gay-marry his own brother at a ceremony, thereby inheriting half the farm as his own brother's legal husband? What then for rural Ireland?

BAN GAY MARRIAGE NOW!

Scenario 2: Gay A and Gay B marry at a 'gay wedding' in Bandon, County Cork. Gay A and Gay B wish to adopt a small child who has a talent for chemistry. Because of The Terrible Laws, they adopt the poor child who is turned gay immediately as a result. The child concocts a formula for gayness in the lab, which can be administered to innocent people simply by spraying it on to the turnstiles at Croke Park. The boy-genius follows through with his plan at a hurling match between Tipperary and Dublin during the 2016 Championship season. On that day alone 80,652 people are turned gay by the potion, except a few GAA gays like Dónal Óg Cusack who are turned straight by mistake, and all these new gays return to their parishes. The country, now probably approaching the nightmare scenario of a gay majority, votes in a new article in the Constitution by referendum, confirming the country of Ireland, the very land itself, to be gay. The island of Ireland, being a gay, now tries to copulate with the island of Britain from behind – sure that's what the gays do, isn't it? – and causes World War 3. The world ends.

BAN GAY MARRIAGE NOW!

Scenario 3: Two gay people get married and live happily ever after, enriching the lives of everyone around them. (We are being sarcastic here, may God forgive us!)

BAN GAY MARRIAGE NOW!
AMEN

The
Connemara Sútra

The Hokey Pokey

No Frills

The Wild Atlantic Way

The Hill 16

Sexting

The Blarney Stone

The Dublin Box Apartment

The Munster Maul

The Breakfast Roll

Chapter 16

The World of Work

For many years, Irish people were forced to emigrate, many thousands leaving to work as navvies on British motorways and many more travelling across the Atlantic where they became 'the hands that felt America'. Sadly, yet again, Irish people are being forced to move overseas to work on 'the sites', most of them as software developers. It is a national tragedy.

In modern Ireland, we do the educational equivalent of fattening up our children like cattle to be exported for slaughter on the international market, where some foreigners get to cut up and feast upon their tasty, well-nourished brains. In a globalized economy, some would say that this is inevitable and even a good thing. Young Irish people get a chance to experience a wider world and new cultures, to spread their wings and broaden their horizons, to not be rained on for a while. Many will bring these experiences back to the land that reared them, returning home with novel business ideas, new and annoying accents, not to mention life partners who aren't white – it's like a massive nation-state software update.

Having said that, there are some Irish people who waste the opportunity. They inevitably move into a six-bedroomed house in Sydney with fourteen other Paddies to survive on a nostalgic diet of Barry's tea and Tayto crisps. There they will stay holed up for a year – careful to avoid any sunlight, cans full of fag butts and redback spiders accumulating around their ankles

214

– with a group consisting mostly of functional alcoholics they were in Transition Year with. They come out from time to time, but only ever at night, to don their county GAA jerseys and cruise Bondi Junction like wide-eyed, albino ghosts.

But wherever you may be, from Timahoe to Timbuktu, it's fair to say that the international world of work now involves many shared experiences.

The Art of the CV

Although most Irish people are now educated to within an inch of their lives, the practice of exaggerating your CV with various professionally themed porkies is alive and well, and almost impossible to resist. Employers, beware!

Stuff Your CV Says	The Truth
I am proficient in Microsoft Word and email.	I know how to turn on a computer. That's about it really.
I have a first-class arts degree in English and History.	I can play acoustic guitar at house parties for many many hours.
I enjoy swimming and reading.	I don't have any hobbies at all, now that I think about it.
February 2014–March 2015: Graphical Reproduction Executive at Wilson, Wilson & Mahony.	I photocopied case files at the old man's legal firm for a year and sold marijuana to my little sister's friends at the weekends.
I'm a hard worker.	Yeah, I clearly worked *really* hard coming up with my list of strong points . . .

Stuff Your CV Says	The Truth
I'm a self-starter.	I cut the wings off flies with a razor blade in my mother's attic. My whereabouts for a whole year during the 1990s cannot be ascertained. I will kill again.
I'm a very creative person.	I'll come up with the most incredible lies when I ring in sick every Monday morning.
I'm reliable and honest.	I'm not reliable or honest.
References available on request.	I'll give you my drug dealer's landline and he'll pretend he's my former boss and say positive things about me when you call him. I'll be doing blowbacks with his girlfriend in the kitchen.

The Office Age

When you do manage to secure that elusive gig, it will most likely take place in an office environment. Offices, for those of you who don't know them, are essentially spiritual gulags that slowly drain your creative energy and lifeblood, page by page, staple by staple. They are built for automatons by automatons to crush the human spirit, set to a soul-destroying soundtrack of photocopiers and clacking keyboards and harmless watercooler banter and OH MY GOOD GOD THE HUMANITY! Having said all that, the Nespresso is great.

Human bodies have evolved over time to have the potential to be fine-tuned and sculpted into perfect persistence hunting machines. Each of us, theoretically, has the raw materials necessary to become a lethal predator over open ground. However, our metabolisms are designed to process fruit and berries and occasional meat, not semi-lethal daily doses of caffeine and party bags of sea-salt-riddled artisan crisps from Somerset. Our limbs react none too well to repeated hours of half-arsed slouching on swivel chairs and nothing in our genetic design could have prepared us for the unique psychological horror of the annual Christmas party. Indeed, if you presented any random Stone Age man with the image of a twentysomething Office Age temp, partitioned away in some cubicle, endlessly filling out spreadsheets, he'd probably smear himself in blood and run screaming towards the nearest available panther to put a stop to it all.

The Co-Workers

If all that wasn't bad enough, you will be penned into these places with a group of co-workers, people whose selection you will have little control over and with whom you will spend more quality time than your own children.

To give you a sense of the type of colleague you might get to enjoy working with in one of these dystopian hellholes, I've interviewed a selection from the US-owned subsidiary Random Technologies, a business based in a technology park 'convenient to the M50' and which definitely exists.

Maria – The Sneezer

Maria is a senior HR officer. She suffers from a freakish range of allergies, which go on throughout the year – hay fever, Christmas sniffles, Easter sinus; there isn't a day that goes by when Maria can't be heard sneezing at full force in the centre of the office, where she rules the roost like a poorly grandmother. Because of these regular and needy nasal expulsions, it is virtually impossible for anyone nearby to get through even a half-hour of work uninterrupted. Maria also expects, nay demands, a sympathetic 'Bless you' after each sneeze and will go on a three-day strop if such a pleasantry isn't forthcoming. Maria's only interest outside work is the TV series *The Good Wife*, which she will discuss scene by scene whether you listen or not. Nobody working at the desk adjacent to Maria's has lasted longer than three months in the job.

Áine – The Temp

Áine has been temping consistently now since the start of the 1990s and it is possible that she has worked in every single office space ever to exist in Dublin. Over the course of that period she has undertaken seventy-six different night and weekend courses including needlework, aqua aerobics, art appreciation, classical music appreciation, appreciation course appreciation and kickboxing. Áine hopes to settle on a career soon, but she seems to get consistently distracted by small irrelevancies. She realizes that perpetual temping is not a perfect situation for anyone entering their early forties and is hoping to settle on a five-year . . . Oh look! There's a little robin on the windowsill! EEEEPPP!

Fergal – The Stationery Hoarder

Over the course of his five years in Random Tech, junior credit controller Fergal has lifted approximately 3,000 reams of paper, 893 pens, 54 staplers, a franking machine and enough toilet paper to travel around the world three times. He is storing all this swag in a shed behind his mother's house and has already flogged half of it on DoneDeal.ie for a relatively sizeable sum. Fergal has been known to spend up to a third of his working week reading *The Herald* on the toilet.

John – *The Transient*

John has just returned from a gap year in Australia and is working in Random Technologies to save up enough money to go back out again '*soon as*'. In fact, John's is more of a gap life than a gap year. He can't conduct a full conversation without sharing a 'When I was in Australia' anecdote: 'The Gold Coast was *wild* man, you'd totally dig it! You've got to live in the bush for a while if you ever get to Australia – it's sweet as.' John has a miniature VW Camper and three Bill Bryson books on his desk to remind him and everybody of his recent travels and he keeps referring to beers as *stubbies*. The entire office is quietly anticipating his return to that great continent, apart from Maria, who hopes to maybe shag him first.

Jennifer – *The Note Leaver*

Office manager and control freak, Jennifer spends much of her working life leaving passive-aggressive notes in the canteen and toilets FAO her fellow employees. These notes contain sentences like 'The coffee machine DOESN'T CLEAN ITSELF!' and 'Please respect your co-workers by LEAVING THIS TOILET AS YOU WOULD EXPECT TO FIND IT!!!' These notes are always followed by a range of smiley faces and assorted emojis to defuse the latent aggression contained within the quiet rage of the text. ☺ xxx

Wayne – The Watercooler Lurker

Head of accounts Wayne has a desk next to the watercooler, forcing him to engage in casual watercooler banter all day, every day for the past five years. It is believed that he has engaged in more pointless banter and fill-the-silence drivel than the presenting teams of *Exposé* and *Saturday Kitchen* combined, stuff like 'So, did you see *America's Next Top Model* last night?' and 'Very *close* today, isn't it?' Wayne may be on the verge of a massive nervous breakdown.

Advertising Andy – The Thirties Bastard

Chief marketing officer Andy considers himself part of one of the 'creative' industries, which would also include television production, online journalism and comedy promotion. Andy will often be seen shuffling around the office in bare feet, with his iPad, brainstorming away in a suit and shirt, but never a tie, a sartorial ensemble commonly referred to as 'The Thirties Bastard'. This is also a perfect description for Andy. Contrary to the strict HR code, Andy has kept a bottle of whiskey in his desk drawer ever since *Mad Men* first aired.

The Work/Life Balance

Do you live to work? Or do you work to live? Thanks to advances in mobile technology, it has become increasingly hard to switch off from the overload of modern communications. Work emails ping in, Twitter notifications ding, another baby photo lands in your Facebook feed . . . Your consciousness is constantly under assault. In modern Ireland it has become vital to recharge and rejuvenate at regular intervals in some primal, back-to-basics way (but do remember to bring a credit card).

Every now and then a digital detox is necessary. Many have resorted to using a classic Nokia 3210, or 'the brick', to reduce their availability to calls and texts. This is the digital equivalent of living in a cave and it is thoroughly recommended.

But you can always physically 'get away from it all', whether it is a weekend in the farthest reaches of Connaught or a day locked in your own basement with your hands tied together. Spiritual retreats are popular – you can now pay top dollar to live like a fifth-century monk in a mud hut off the Irish coast to get away from the workaday buzz. You can even climb Croagh Patrick in your bare and bloodied feet, often with Enda Kenny roaring 'You can do it!' from behind.

Also, Ireland is absolutely awash with hotel lodge and spas, those retreats for the working worried, which will cost you an arm, a leg and many of the muscles around your shoulder area. With names like Heather Lake and The Ebony (see, don't you feel relaxed just reading them?) these buildings will mostly consist of seaweed, synthesizer and an intense 'dripping' sensation you won't be able to shake for days. The staff, dressed in blinding white no doubt, will be a mix of pathologically violent masseurs and receptionists made up mostly of eyebrow. They will calmly guide you, in that soothing lodge-and-spa voice of theirs, through the total detoxification of your mind, body and spirit as well as the complete liberation of much of your disposable income.

So go on. You know you deserve it.

Chapter 17

Property and Pensions

When the early Irish arrived, they brought with them a housing culture that proudly survives to this day. In fact, evidence has been found to suggest that within a decade of these people arriving the property market around Dublin had become dangerously overheated. Many of the huge monuments excavated around the dry-stone walls of their unsophisticated mud dwellings were actually 'For Sale' stones. Additionally, more recent discoveries of several Neolithic burial sites reveal the remains of couples that appear to have been viciously clubbed to death in violent attacks. Archaeologists now believe these vicious murders occurred at a, presumably oversubscribed, cave viewing around what is now the Shrewsbury Road

area of Ballsbridge. This obsession with property, how to get your foot on the ladder and the ancient Irish tradition of gazumping are themes that have recurred again and again throughout the course of Irish history.

Castle Duckrent

What's the most effective way to make people obsess over something for centuries? Keep taking it off them over the course of centuries. This is exactly what British colonialists did. If they had come in and taken all our ducks, for instance, and forbidden the Irish ownership of ducks, we might now be running a predominantly duck-centred economy. Many people would dress like ducks, duck would replace the spud as the main food staple and *The Irish Times* would have a whole section dedicated to the sale and acquisition of various types of overpriced, under-decorated ducks, probably poorly insulated with the wrong type of feather. After eight hundred years of dispossession at the hands of English landlords – the accepted mortal enemies of the Irish – we then had to suffer at the hands of the only thing in the universe known to be categorically worse than that – the Irish landlord.

The typical Irish landlord is about fifty-eight and lives around the North Circular Road area of Dublin. As well as a comb-over large enough to set sail out of Dublin Bay, his pants will generally be held up with twine and he will often sport a distinctly nasal voice, evolved over decades in order to perfectly deliver sentences like 'I'm afraid I won't be aaaaaaable to refuuuund your depooooooosit because the bliiiiiiinds are brooooooooooooken' and 'I'm soooooorry I didn't caaaaall to fiiiiix the heeeeeeating, I was awaaaaaaaaaay hoooooome in

Monaghaaaaaaan. Did you enjooooy the Christmaaaaaaas any-waaaaaaay?' Even though this man might look, act and smell like a hobo, he will own at least ten properties around central Dublin, each one more decrepit than the last, and is a paper millionaire.

As a result, renting in Ireland is about as secure as taking a cargo ship down the coast of Somalia. Most of our apartments are really only family-sized if you're talking about small families of herring. Also, it shouldn't be forgotten that renting in Ireland is a massive social taboo. 'My son is in Dublin and he's renting' is often said with the same solemn disappointment as 'My son is in Dublin and copulates with pigeons in public for money'.

Saving for a Deposit

Inevitably, exhausted tenants will give in and try to get their foot on 'the ladder', a beanstalk-type construction that spirals up into the clouds over Ireland and has as many snakes to fall down as rungs to climb up.

What is the first step to getting on a magic beanstalk? Why, amass a lottery-sized sum of magic beans, of course! This is commonly referred to by people in the industry as The Deposit. Here are some handy tips to help you get your hands on those elusive funds.

1. Find a Benefactor

If you were lucky enough to have been born into the 1 per cent or you're the offspring of, for example, a recently disgraced banker, money won't be a problem. A diverse portfolio of investments, their massive pension and many lucrative engagements on the US speaking circuit will ensure a steady flow of lucre for all the family. However, trying to be born into one of these families, after the fact, could prove difficult. Time travel is expensive. 'Marrying up' is possible, but that could prove awkward and divisive if, say, you're already married. Adult adoption, on the other hand, is a route worth considering. If you're a man, why not attempt to gain the maternal affections of a lonely property developer's wife whose husband is 'away on business for a little while'? This could be done in a number of ways, e.g. by volunteering to do a spot of gardening or paper shredding. Make sure to cheerfully whistle the arias of Schubert as you roughly prune back the rose bushes with those manly arms. Then, when she is at her weakest, perhaps after an afternoon sherry or a poor morning on the tennis court, hit her with your carefully scripted sob story about how you're stuck in a houseshare with an unhappy wife and thirteen bicycle couriers. Look suitably ashamed as you admit you haven't seen the inside of a restaurant since *Raw* was cancelled. Then, after a particularly pregnant pause, drop the 'renting is dead money' line, before bursting into tears.

Women can employ a similar tactic, but it requires less effort. In fact, finding a sugar daddy has never been easier. For instance, you could try walking up to any large Mercedes in traffic and make the driver an offer he can't refuse. And Bob will, quite literally, be your uncle.

2. Harvest Your Organs

If outright prostitution is a road you do not wish to travel down, then why not look to some of your other untapped resources closer to home? According to the Internet, we only use 10 per cent of our brains. Anyone who has spent any time at all on YouTube comment sections will know this to be an incontrovertible fact. But perhaps it's time to liberate that equity sitting there in the old noggin. Do you really need *all* of that brain in your day-to-day work? It's well known that Russian oligarchs will pay top dollar for human brains, a delicacy now in many London restaurants. Don't stop there – most of us have the benefit of a spare kidney, which is sitting there, unused and hoovering up resources, like a West Kerry holiday home. Get rid.

3. Start a Ponzi Scheme

Many of you might have gained priceless experience in this area during the communionism period or the Celtic Tiger. For those of you that haven't, it's pretty simple.

Have you considered emailing your friends and colleagues about an opportunity that will guarantee them a whopping 50 per cent return on their investment? Can you do a convincing Nigerian accent? Do you own a crown? Is this the script of a radio advert? If you have answered yes to any of these questions then why not set up a Ponzi scheme? The trick is to pay off early investors with the money from new investors and siphon off a little for yourself at every stage of the pyramid. Then, suddenly, BAM! You've up and made off with all the money! (Madoff: get it? GET IT?) However, you need to know when to cash in your chips. If you get on the ladder of a Ponzi scheme too late, you will bear the brunt of the scam yourself. Just ask anyone who bought a house in Ireland between 2007 and 2010.

4. *Saving*

This is a pretty bizarre one, I admit, but bear with me here. If you are lucky enough to be able to spare around four hundred euros at the end of every month, it would only take you twelve and a half years to save sixty thousand euros for that two-bed terraced ex-council house in Stoneybatter in which you can theoretically swing a cat (subject to planning and assuming zero inflation in the meantime). If you start saving now, you could be in the door and decorating this side of fifty. (If you're already fifty and reading this, sorry, you've missed the boat. However, I do know a guy on the North Circular Road who's looking for tenants . . . Cash only. Wink wink.)

The Viewing

Now that you've begged, borrowed and probably stolen a little cash for a deposit and scored that elusive mortgage, the next step in the game of Irish life is to peruse some gaffs. This can be done with the help of websites like Daft and MyHome, where you can filter the absolute shitboxes from the mere shitholes and hone in on the areas within your price range (Achill Island, most likely). Invariably the house will include GFCH and all mod cons (door, walls and electricity) as well as 'ample storage'. An ample is a rare Portuguese variant on the satsuma. These places will generally only hold a single ample. A word of warning: the photos on these sites cannot always be depended on. Rumour has it that many well-oiled estate agents com-missioned NASA to design and custom-build wide-angle lenses during the Celtic Tiger that can make a four-foot-by-three-foot former toilet look like the sprawling vestibule of a

Venetian palace. So it's always worth paying a visit before you buy.

When you do choose to visit, don't expect to see the place on your own. You'll most definitely have company. You see the victims of this reality every weekend – ashen-faced couples, sleeplessly wandering around oversubscribed property viewings like desperate punters trying to get in their last orders, pleading with aloof estate agents like it could possibly make a difference.

Did we learn nothing at all from the David McWilliams books? What about all those documentaries with the foreboding soundtracks from 2009? Programmes with horrendously provocative titles like *Property Armageddon*, *You'll Never Eat Again* and *Prime Time Investigates*?

Meh, not really.

So here are some hard-learnt tips for those of you brave enough to venture out to a property viewing. After this lesson, you may not own the property, but I guarantee you, you'll have totally owned the viewing.

1. The Loudmouth

One of the best ways to intimidate fellow buyers is to march around the property, loudly announcing your plans for its renovation, as if it's already in the bag. 'Would this coalshed convert into a changing room for the pool I wonder, Bernard?' 'Certainly, dear. Also we should restore all the original features of the house – the floorboards, the wooden beams, the fireplaces, even the aul' fella who used to own it. We should exhume him and sit him in the armchair by the fire there.' 'Definitely! How rustic! And I'm thinking a scheme incorporating taupe for the landing.'

2. The Scaremonger

This is one of the most effective techniques. Remember, capitalism has conspired to drum all the other buyers into a state of almost perpetual anxiety. Freaking them out even more is a sure-fire way to eliminate some competition. Remember to loudly enquire about the potential for asbestos in the ceilings. Make sure to cough uncontrollably after you've said this. Then, loudly whisper to your partner on the stairs any combination of the following words: 'murders', 'unsolved', 'meat cleaver' and 'haunted, I reckon'.

3. Trojan Fridge

A classic, this. When nobody's looking, throw a load of cheese and vegetables into the fridge and unplug it. Everybody knows that it's nigh-on impossible to view a house without giving in to the temptation to open the fridge. Any subsequent viewings will be interesting, to say the least.

4. The Expert

A close cousin of The Scaremonger, only a simple bit of fancy dress required for this one, namely a hard hat, yellow hi-vis vest, measuring tape and a mobile phone. Busily march around the property like you're doing a bit of consulting for a potential buyer. Tap on the walls while frowning. Loudly bellowing into your phone using any of the following phrases should do the trick: 'death trap', 'pyrite', 'money pit' or 'Dermot Bannon started crying yesterday when I showed him the photos'.

If these pointers don't give you an edge, I don't know what will.

Flatpackers Anonymous

Now that you've got yourself on the property ladder, it's time to start decking the place out a bit. Give your new home a touch of 'you'. Well, what could be more you than a generic piece of flatpack furniture from an airport-sized Scandinavian furniture outlet?

Human beings alive today are lucky enough to be the next in a long genetic line that stretches back to the very greatest masters of architecture and construction. Those fearless visionaries who pushed against the boundaries of engineering, shaping metal, stone and glass to make tunnels that cut through vast mountains, skyscrapers that touch the heavens and bridges that span mighty rivers.

In 3200 BC, it is estimated that a team of over three hundred workers would have toiled for thirty years to amass the two hundred thousand tonnes of earth, mud and stone that make up Newgrange. In New York in the late 1800s, the Brooklyn Bridge took more than a decade to build, with its imposing towers of limestone, granite and Rosendale cement. Around thirty men were killed during its construction, including its designer, as they drilled deeper and deeper into the East River bedrock.

Last March, I constructed an Ikea Brimnes chest of three drawers, using: 12 x plastic screws, 24 x smaller metal screws, 24 x wooden sticky things, 4 x iron bendy yokes and 1 x Allen key. It took me one hour and thirty-seven minutes to complete, and during construction I hurt my finger quite badly.

To get to the point, before this lumbering introduction collapses under the overbearing weight of its own assembly, I'm not a DIY expert.

My knowledge of fundamental engineering concepts is scant. Tolerance coning, weight distribution, metal fatigue – all I really know about these terms is that they come up when you google 'fundamental engineering concepts'. Likewise, I'm not really on top of all the boring health and safety stuff. Will this thing really electrocute me if I poke at it with a fork? Superglue and eyelids: what's the latest research? Hey, I wonder what happens if I eat these? That whole world is about as alien and bewildering to me as *Strictly Come Dancing*. However, in my defence, there are some signs of progress. I've learnt to skilfully dip a brush into a can of paint and artfully apply it to a wall, shelf or ceiling. I can effortlessly stick those cheap plastic hooks on to the backs of toilet doors.

So when those Ikea flatpack challenges come around, I tackle them with all the seriousness and self-importance of someone embarking on the Hoover Dam project. It's basically a rare opportunity for me to grunt, curse and scratch my arse in the way all men were originally designed to do.

Firstly, I always read the instructions carefully. I realize that this isn't a very Irish thing to do. The natural inclination would be to tear into it like a Celtic Tiger cowboy builder firing up an apartment. But I go 'full Swedish' – I count out and carefully display all the fixtures and fittings. I line up all my tools (screwdriver, hammer) like a surgeon preparing to transplant a kidney. I make sure to study carefully all those confusing diagrams, with the little Ikea man with the beer belly, that include reminders like:

DO lay out all the components on cardboard so as not to mark the wood
DON'T shove the screwdriver up your nostrils
DO get an adult to help you with the scissors
DON'T lie on the floor in tears for three hours, mourning the death of your youth

Thankfully, the great Ikea trick is that even a drunk idiot with penguins for hands couldn't really get these flatpacks wrong. They are generally designed so well, without any chance of any pesky creativity creeping into the mix, that you end up with a spanking-new piece of furniture that looks exactly like the photo on the website.

It's then that the disproportionate pride kicks in. That pathetic 'Look what I did, dear' half-hour of macho smugness that occurs as you survey your wondrous creation. The feeling men used to only get, I presume, after starting a war or killing a squirrel with their bare hands.

But I never look back for too long, me. The next project? Hemnes double-bed frame with matching lockers – bring it on!

The Pensions Timebomb

This week a man visited me in my house. He had grey hair, a grey suit, grey shoes, grey socks and a grey face, so I can only presume he was visiting from the afterlife. Which would make sense, because he wanted to talk to me about pensions.

You might remember those radio adverts from a few years back where sixty-year-old you is haranguing thirty-year-old you about being more responsible: 'Dear thirty-year-old me, you're a big fat waste of space. Look at you there, sprawled out on the sofa waiting for another takeaway, you absolute disgrace to your ancestry. Why are you smiling? Don't you know you're going to DIE? Bad things often happen to good people, you know. Like DEATH. Oh, and by the way, if you don't start a pension now, by 2050 you'll end up destitute and penniless, shivering miserably in some futuristic tower block straight out of Terry Gilliam's brain. That's if you don't DIE in the meantime.'

Anyway, you get my drift. The grey man's pitch was similar in tone.

Ads like this are always bloody on. If I wasn't horrified enough on my commute to the office, what with the media updating me on the ever-present threat of international terrorism, black-eyed ghost children, leaves on the tracks, etc. etc., I'm sure to be buckled over in panic by the time I'm guiltily tucking into my morning pastry.

It's got to the stage where I'm half-expecting sixty-year-old me to actually start haunting me. Any night now he'll be sitting at the end of my bed, sagging and toothless, pleading with me to start flossing again. And to cut back on the pastries.

Now unlike, off the top of my head, any former cabinet minister, I'm not going to receive a huge windfall from the state once I retire. Like most people of my generation, it's likely that I'll have to work well into my nineties, as some sort of a grandad-slave to my hipster grandchildren. So I've tried to be responsible. I've looked at all the basic options: PRSAs (too confusing), MRSAs (too infectious) and even MDMAs (too psychotropic). It's a frickin' minefield.

See, from what I can gather, the private-pensions system works like this:

1 You get tax relief when you put a certain amount towards a pension every month.

2 This money is then placed into the hands of a clever person in an office somewhere in a building made of glass and they invest it wisely, because they love you and they want to protect you and your family for the future. They have a kindly face and an unthreatening name, like Alison, and they own a holiday home in Connemara with fantastic stonework.

3 You can't touch the money until you're older than Santa. If you do, you incur severe penalties, like having one of your limbs removed with an angle grinder.

4 The government takes a little bit of it every year, called a levy, which they use to buy chocolate.

5 The government may increase this levy at a later stage, because there's no money left to fix the roads and they've run out of chocolate.

6 As you get older, the money gets moved into 'safer' asset classes like shares in Irish banks or government bonds.

7 The morning of your retirement, at age eighty-seven, as you cheerfully dump that last bucket of medical waste into the river as part of your nightshift at the cloning farm, the global financial system goes into another meltdown and you lose the lot.

8 You are unable to reach kindly Alison, who is sitting on a yacht or a spaceship reading *Fifty Shades of Grey* and who probably looks like she is twenty-five, having discovered some sort of elixir that stops the ageing process.

9 You die and spend the rest of eternity howling into a vortex with the black-eyed ghost children.

However, there are some practical solutions for those of you in the same boat. So, after countless minutes of research, here are five simple tips you can put into practice TODAY.*

The Five Roads to a Secure Old Age™

1 Marry a teacher.

2 Marry a Kardashian.

3 Teach a Kardashian.

4 Move to Kardashia.

5 Join the Gardaí and infiltrate the Kardashians.

Here's hoping these tips will help you secure your future and that you'll have an absolute langerload of funds in place to enjoy those golden years.

---

* This section should not be taken as financial advice. It was written by an idiot who got a C in Leaving Cert Accounting. The value of your investments may fall as well as rise. Kardashia is not an official state yet. Other terms and conditions apply but in all fairness you've all stopped reading by now anyway because this is the small print.

Chapter 18

Death

A **recent survey** conducted by the Central Statistics Office estimates that 100 per cent of the readers of this book are going to succumb to death at least once over the course of their lifetime. That's a fairly shocking statistic, in any man's language.

The breadth and colour and carnival of your preceding life are likely, unfortunately, to be reflected in the potential manner of your snuffing it. You could fall off a ladder while pruning a hedge. You could succumb to cancer. You could get decapitated in a road bowling incident. You could be hit by a bus. You could be hit by a bus, get up again, only to get hit by a second bus because they always come in twos. You could overdose on Viagra, fair play to you. Spiders could lay eggs in your brain causing you to join Young Fine Gael and you might inadvertently end up killing yourself with austerity. You could get a job in the oil industry and die slowly inside. You might even die of a Tuesday.

So, you'd sometimes wonder, what was it all for?

Over the course of your lifetime, you will have survived conception, birth, nappies, the miserable teens, the roaring twenties, the slightly depressing thirties, the work-your-arse-off forties and the gnawing worry of your fifties. Before you know it you'll have lived through the swinging sixties and it will soon be time for your seventies and even eighties when you'll, in all likelihood, be back in the nappies again, but at least listening to Michael Bublé.

As an Irish person, you'll have put up with a fair bit of trouble in those years: desperate, unpredictable weather; about thirty recessions; ten currency changes; twenty World Cups; fifty-seven dysfunctional coalition governments; and the FAI. You'll have emigrated and immigrated and emigrated again.

You'll be absolutely knackered.

Top Ten Irish Deathbed Regrets

1 I wish I hadn't worked so hard.

2 I wish I spent more time with family.

3 I spent way too much time with my family.

4 I shouldn't have been so hard on Roy Keane.

5 Having said that, Mick McCarthy shouldn't have let loose on him like that in front of everyone, in all fairness.

6 I wish I had brought a cushion, this trolley is fucking killing me.

7 Why did I spend most of my thirties in Ikea?

8 Eircom shares – doh!

13 Should have knuckled down more in Maths class.

10 Spent too much time making stupid lists.

Not to worry. Hopefully you'll have time to say your goodbyes and settle your affairs before you go. In all likelihood, though, you'll be spending a good part of those last, precious days frantically trying to delete embarrassing stuff about yourself from the Internet. There is one last thing to look forward to, however, one final swansong, even if you're not around to see it: your funeral. The crowning achievement of any Irish life.

Few are held in higher esteem in Ireland than those who have recently ceased to exist. It doesn't matter what odious deeds you may have been responsible for over the course of your days and it counts not a jot how many of your fellow citizens you sold down the river in that dodgy time-share scheme that went belly-up. For the immediate future at least, you are 'the salt of the earth' who 'had a good innings' and 'your like will never be seen again'.

Ar dheis Dé go raibh a h-anam.

It's probably a bit of a cliché at this stage, but we do death very well in Ireland. If the Germans engineer great cars and the Swiss make great clocks, nobody expires like we do.

We're world-champion clog-poppers.

The true meaning of the word 'community' can be seen in all its Irish glory in the way we celebrate the death of a loved one, or even someone we actively despised for that matter. It's fair to say that we don't really do funeral commemorations like other cultures, where you go quietly into that good night and are respectfully sent off by a few close well-wishers and relatives. You see these a lot in England, lonely affairs for the most part, with a few neighbours huddled around a coffin, a sense of embarrassment at being confronted by such a thing as your own mortality and the subtle waft of Marmite moving through the awkwardness.

In Ireland, a funeral is much closer in scale and atmosphere to a small music festival, Body & Soul if you will. It usually runs over three days – the removal kicking things off, followed by the funeral, which is the main event and then the burial. For the real hardcore, the family will most likely invite you back to the hotel after for refreshments. This is the equivalent of getting into the staff rave in the woods after the festival is over.

The mourners will arrive to the church in droves, trailing around graves and huddling under trees, fag butts accumulating around them. There will be a hushed silence. The only sound you'll likely hear is the pocking of hearse tyres on gravel and a bit of sniffling. Smiling isn't on at all.

At an Irish funeral, it is customary for the line of sympathizers to grow almost unimaginably long, as people turn up to 'show their face'. Famously, at one funeral in Donegal, the parade of handshakers extended out so far that three further members of the mourning family had passed away by the time the line had finished, by which point the sympathizers had to just turn back round, return to the end of the line and start all over again.

Everyone wants to pay their respects. But they also have a second important goal and civic duty – to collectively distract the grieving family from their sorrow and ease their private burden in the most public way. This is done in a time-honoured tradition that involves slowly but surely breaking all the bones in their hands. And it works. There's no amount of grief ten broken fingers won't take your mind off. As this act of considerate violence is gradually administered by the throngs, you will notice the people engaging you on various emotional levels as they pass along.

Some, often women of advancing years, will make full eye contact and say with great warmth, 'I'm so very sorry. I hope you are all okay'. They then move on, respectfully. But you also get the more hurried, half-embarrassed 'Sorry for your troubles' handshakes as the person half-glances at you out of the sides of their eyes before moving along the line – young men often; it wasn't easy for them, but they did it. Of course there are those who more or less high-five you as they speed past, grunting 'Srrrytrble', before storming out the door to get home in time to milk the cows. Who's to say they meant it any less though? The cows won't milk themselves like.

After about 3,400 handshakes, you pause for a minute, perhaps applying ice to the injured area, and try to take it all in – you see the parade of familiar and not-so-familiar faces, the neighbours, the old GAA compatriots, aged headmasters and codgers you presumed were dead a decade ago, now edging like turtles down the aisle. You survey the shameless politicians going to shameless lengths to make themselves shamelessly visible before the congregation – there's a man (or woman) with a plan! And of course, there are the people you don't know at all, many of them funeral crashers who keep a keen eye on RIP.ie, constant mourners who travel around from funeral to funeral, in a constant state of grief and peckishness, their singular ambition being to get back to the hotel for the free food.

*

And you soon realize – there it is! In all its glory. Ireland.

I can think of no place I'd rather be.

It really is absolutely batshit.

Backword

You don't need me to tell you that Ireland has had it pretty tough during the second decade of the twenty-first century.

The economy was brought to its knees by the synchronized fuckwittery of a coterie of gombeen politicians, swashbuckling property developers, unregulated bankers, hare-brained Euro gurus, and the wide-eyed collusion of an aspirational population desperate for even a small pinch of prosperity after countless dark decades of slowly accumulating Bovril.

What happened in Ireland really was the perfect storm of converging interests – a veritable Axis of Eeejitry. After the Smeg-riddled waking dream that was the Celtic Tiger came crashing down to earth, the country was further humiliated into an international bailout by the Troika, the terrifying three-some made up of the EU, the ECB and the KLF (who burn money for fun), which had us pay, all told, 42% of the total cost of the European banking crisis – around €9,000 per person.

That's a hell of a lot of strawberry Cornettos.

Over the course of a historical eye blink, Ireland went from being poster boys for subsistence living and rogue building to poster boys for hyper-capitalist globalization, unstoppable techno-Gaels who swaggered across the financial world stage spitting rainbows and shitting pots of gold, before going back to being poster boys for subsistence living, rogue building and, indeed, for Austerity™ itself.

It would be great, for a while at least, not to be featured on any more posters. And perhaps not have so many boys in charge.

Now that 'the recovery' has apparently 'taken hold', we've started raking and stoking it all up again, attempting to settle old scores and wag fingers in toothless banking inquiries and lengthy court cases, which only ever seem to result in lawyers getting richer and old dudes in Mercs sheepishly returning to golf courses whilst sarcastically humming 'My Way'.

I don't know about you, but I've sort of had it . . .

We've each got about eighty years of life on this earth, if we're lucky. You have to ask yourself, do you really want to spend *all* those eighty years stewing over past failures, whipping yourself up into a tizzy on Twitter or furiously texting drive-time radio shows about how those bastard banksters should all be jailed before repeatedly head-butting the steering wheel and knocking yourself out? This was how I spent much of 2010.

And it's not just Ireland we have to worry about either. Polar ice caps are slowly going the way of Offaly hurling. Astronomers reckon the universe itself is gradually running out of energy and dying. Jeremy Clarkson, it seems, will be on our screens for some time to come.

There are so many reasons to think negatively about the future.

However – and I'm not unlike Meatloaf here – I won't do that.

It might not be very trendy, especially in this era of 24-hour rolling rage, but let me for a minute take a glass-half-full position.

We are but a small, battered island nation off the edge of Western Europe, only recently emerging from the fog of an often-brutal history. It also happens to be one of the most beautiful places in the world. The people, generally, are sound. The surf is great. The monkfish is handsome.

International capitalism insists on quantifying our progress economically, prescribing that we must grow and grow and grow until we get so bloated and sweaty we simply crash through the Earth's core and out through China. Maybe, just maybe, we could develop the confidence to shape our own future, to be brave enough to swim against this tide, to stand up for the things that work for us now and which we should cherish. Things like our strong community bonds; the widespread and proud diaspora; our fine music and cultural heritage; our thriving sports; Paul McGrath's reading of the game; Irish cheese; the sun setting over the Aran Islands; Banshee Bones; the fact that Kate Bush's mother was from Waterford; our world-beating funerals . . . I could go on.

Allow me to totally lose the run of myself here. By 2050, why couldn't Ireland stand out in Europe as a beacon for sustainable living? Why couldn't we enjoy a three-day working week and extend the Electric Picnic to run for the entire summer? Could we not dream of a fairer, more equal society, celebrating the diversity of all the people who can enjoy an amazing indigenous food culture, housing estates that aren't haunted and a recent history free of boy bands? Might we not foster a new political culture where an engaged, passionate citizenry, not 'taxpayers' or 'stakeholders', but *citizens*, can't be so easily bought off by civil war politics, which has proven to have all the long-term vision of a pig which has recently discovered peanut butter on its genitals?

Why on earth not?

The wind might be against us but I have a feeling we might just do it.

Acknowledgements

First of all I'd like to thank God, my producers the Weinstein Brothers and in particular, Jack Nicholson who I now consider not only a colleague but a close personal fr—

Oh, you mean my *book* acknowledgements?

Right so . . .

Thanks to Brian Langan, Eoin McHugh and all at Transworld for their passion for this project from the outset. Your sage advice was priceless throughout.

Thanks to anyone who has ever followed me on Twitter, or retweeted one of my jokes, or indeed anyone who anonymously hurled abuse at me from their sofa.

Thanks to Darren Smith at Kite Entertainment for his continued support in my dream of never having to get a real job.

Thanks to Ian Kenny whose wonderful illustrations I am so proud to have in this book. Thanks also to Aidan O'Donovan for all his help and advice.

Thanks to my Mam, Dad and my sister Emma, the best family I could have ever wished for.

Thanks in particular to my beautiful wife Maura for all her

love, support and good humour, and for keeping me going when I hit the many walls, blocks, barriers and other assorted obstacles along the way.

Oh, and thanks to little Leo, who made 2015 the best year ever.